Social Security

Social Security

Paul Ruschmann, J.D.
& Maryanne Nasiatka

SERIES EDITOR
Alan Marzilli, M.A., J.D.

CHELSEA HOUSE
An Infobase Learning Company

Social Security

Chelsea House
An imprint of Infobase Learning
132 West 31st Street
New York, NY 10001

Library of Congress Cataloging-in-Publication Data
Ruschmann, Paul.
Social security / Paul Ruschmann, Maryanne Nasiatka.
p. cm. — (Point/counterpoint series)
Includes bibliographical references and index.
ISBN 978-1-60413-775-0 (hardcover)
1. Social security. I. Nasiatka, Maryanne. II. Title. III. Series.

HD7091.R887 2011
368.4'300973—dc22

                              2010026478

Chelsea House books are available at special discounts when purchased in bulk quantities for businesses, associations, institutions, or sales promotions. Please call our Special Sales Department in New York at (212) 967-8800 or (800) 322-8755.

You can find Chelsea House on the World Wide Web at http://www.chelseahouse.com.

Text design by Keith Trego
Cover design by Alicia Post
Composition by EJB Publishing Services
Cover printed by Bang Printing, Brainerd, MN
Book printed and bound by Bang Printing, Brainerd, MN
Date printed: March 2011
Printed in the United States of America

10 9 8 7 6 5 4 3 2 1

Alan Marzilli, M.A., J.D.
Birmingham, Alabama

The POINT/COUNTERPOINT series offers the reader a greater understanding of some of the most controversial issues in contemporary American society—issues such as capital punishment, immigration, gay rights, and gun control. We have looked for the most contemporary issues and have included topics—such as the controversies surrounding "blogging"—that we could not have imagined when the series began.

In each volume, the author has selected an issue of particular importance and set out some of the key arguments on both sides of the issue. Why study both sides of the debate? Maybe you have yet to make up your mind on an issue, and the arguments presented in the book will help you to form an opinion. More likely, however, you will already have an opinion on many of the issues covered by the series. There is always the chance that you will change your opinion after reading the arguments for the other side. But even if you are firmly committed to an issue—for example, school prayer or animal rights—reading both sides of the argument will help you to become a more effective advocate for your cause. By gaining an understanding of opposing arguments, you can develop answers to those arguments.

Perhaps more importantly, listening to the other side sometimes helps you see your opponent's arguments in a more human way. For example, Sister Helen Prejean, one of the nation's most visible opponents of capital punishment, has been deeply affected by her interactions with the families of murder victims. By seeing the families' grief and pain, she understands much better why people support the death penalty, and she is able to carry out her advocacy with a greater sensitivity to the needs and beliefs of death penalty supporters.

The books in the series include numerous features that help the reader to gain a greater understanding of the issues. Real-life examples illustrate the human side of the issues. Each chapter also includes excerpts from relevant laws, court cases, and other material, which provide a better foundation for understanding the arguments. The volumes contain citations to relevant sources of law and information, and an appendix guides the reader through the basics of legal research, both on the Internet and in the library. Today, through free Web sites, it is easy to access legal documents, and these books might give you ideas for your own research.

Studying the issues covered by the POINT/COUNTERPOINT series is more than an academic activity. The issues described in the books affect all of us as citizens. They are the issues that today's leaders debate and tomorrow's leaders will decide. While all of the issues covered in the POINT/COUNTERPOINT series are controversial today, and will remain so for the foreseeable future, it is entirely possible that the reader might one day play a central role in resolving the debate. Today it might seem that some debates—such as capital punishment and abortion—will never be resolved.

However, our nation's history is full of debates that seemed as though they never would be resolved, and many of the issues are now well settled—at least on the surface. In the nineteenth century, abolitionists met with widespread resistance to their efforts to end slavery. Ultimately, the controversy threatened the union, leading to the Civil War between the northern and southern states. Today, while a public debate over the merits of slavery would be unthinkable, racism persists in many aspects of society.

Similarly, today nobody questions women's right to vote. Yet at the beginning of the twentieth century, suffragists fought public battles for women's voting rights, and it was not until the passage of the Nineteenth Amendment in 1920 that the legal right of women to vote was established nationwide.

What makes an issue controversial? Often, controversies arise when most people agree that there is a problem but disagree about the best way to solve it. There is little argument that poverty is a major problem in the United States, especially in inner cities and rural areas. Yet, people disagree vehemently about the best way to address the problem. To some, the answer is social programs, such as welfare, food stamps, and public housing. However, many argue that such subsidies encourage dependence on government benefits while unfairly penalizing those who work and pay taxes, and that the real solution is to require people to support themselves.

American society is in a constant state of change, and sometimes modern practices clash with what many consider to be "traditional values," which are often rooted in conservative political views or religious beliefs. Many blame high crime rates, and problems such as poverty, illiteracy, and drug use on the breakdown of the traditional family structure of a married mother and father raising their children. Since the "sexual revolution" of the 1960s and 1970s, sparked in part by the widespread availability of the birth control pill, marriage rates have declined, and the number of children born outside of marriage has increased. The sexual revolution led to controversies over birth control, sex education, and other issues, most prominently abortion. Similarly, the gay rights movement has been challenged as a threat to traditional values. While many gay men and lesbians want to have the same right to marry and raise families as heterosexuals, many politicians and others have challenged gay marriage and adoption as a threat to American society.

Sometimes, new technology raises issues that we have never faced before, and society disagrees about the best solution. Are people free to swap music online, or does this violate the copyright laws that protect songwriters and musicians' ownership of the music that they create? Should scientists use "genetic engineering" to create new crops that are resistant to disease and pests and produce more food, or is it too risky to use a laboratory to create plants that nature never intended? Modern medicine has continued to increase the average lifespan—which is now 77 years, up from under 50 years at the beginning of the twentieth century—but many people are now choosing to die in comfort rather than living with painful ailments in their later years. For doctors, this presents an ethical dilemma: should they allow their patients to die? Should they assist patients in ending their own lives painlessly?

Perhaps the most controversial issues are those that implicate a Constitutional right. The Bill of Rights—the first 10 Amendments to the U.S. Constitution—spells out some of the most fundamental rights that distinguish our democracy from other nations with fewer freedoms. However, the sparsely worded document is open to interpretation, with each side saying that the Constitution is on their side. The Bill of Rights was meant to protect individual liberties; however, the needs of some individuals clash with society's needs. Thus, the Constitution often serves as a battleground between individuals and government officials seeking to protect society in some way. The First Amendment's guarantee of "freedom of speech" leads to some very difficult questions. Some forms of expression—such as burning an American flag—lead to public outrage, but are protected by the First Amendment. Other types of expression that most people find objectionable—such as child pornography—are not protected by the Constitution. The question is not only where to draw the line, but whether drawing lines around constitutional rights threatens our liberty.

The Bill of Rights raises many other questions about individual rights and societal "good." Is a prayer before a high school football game an "establishment of religion" prohibited by the First Amendment? Does the Second Amendment's promise of "the right to bear arms" include concealed handguns? Does stopping and frisking someone standing on a known drug corner constitute "unreasonable search and seizure" in violation of the Fourth Amendment? Although the U.S. Supreme Court has the ultimate authority in interpreting the U.S. Constitution, its answers do not always satisfy the public. When a group of nine people—sometimes by a five-to-four vote—makes a decision that affects hundreds of millions of others, public outcry can be expected. For example, the Supreme Court's 1973 ruling in *Roe v. Wade* that abortion is protected by the Constitution did little to quell the debate over abortion.

Whatever the root of the controversy, the books in the POINT/ COUNTERPOINT series seek to explain to the reader the origins of the debate, the current state of the law, and the arguments on either side of the debate. Our hope in creating this series is that readers will be better informed about the issues facing not only our politicians, but all of our nation's citizens, and become more actively involved in resolving these debates, as voters, concerned citizens, journalists, or maybe even elected officials.

Millions of American families struggle to get by on a day-to-day basis. For these families, the idea of saving for retirement seems beyond reach. Even those who have saved diligently for retirement have watched their investments lose a substantial portion of their value since the market crashes of 2008. With each paycheck, however, employers and employees pay into the Social Security system, which pays money to people who reach retirement age or become disabled. This system has been a cornerstone of American society for decades, as protection against another Great Depression. Despite its durability, the system is not as strong as it used to be. People live longer, and an increasing number of people are retiring as people who were born during the post-World War II "baby boom" reach retirement age. There are serious questions about how the system will fund the retirement of young workers who are paying into the system today. This volume examines some of the controversies surrounding the Social Security system. There is a factual debate as to whether predictions of Social Security's demise are rational or based on fear. Others debate whether "forced savings" like Social Security is a wise social policy. In recent years, the debate has increasingly focused on "privatizing" Social Security, so that people are able to make their own decisions on how to invest their Social Security accounts, rather than relying on the system.

The Story of Social Security

F or nineteenth-century workers, retirement was a luxury. A fortunate few—including military veterans, railroad workers, and government employees—had employer-provided pension plans. Other workers, however, had to rely on their savings; help from family members; and, if all else failed, public charity. Because most Americans had no source of income in their post-working years, they ran a high risk of falling into poverty. In 1912, L.W. Squier, the author of *Old Age Dependency in the United States*, described what most older Americans faced:

> After the age of sixty has been reached, the transition from non-dependence to dependence is an easy stage— property gone, friends passed away or removed, relatives become few, ambition collapsed, only a few short years left to live, with death a final and welcome end

to it all—such conclusions inevitably sweep the wage-earners from the class of hopeful independent citizens into that of the helpless poor.[1]

What we know today as the modern "social safety net"—programs that provide government aid to citizens who suffer serious financial setbacks—originated in Germany in the 1880s. Otto von Bismarck, the German chancellor, introduced old-age pensions; government-provided health insurance; and compensation for disabled persons, workers injured while on the job, and children of workers who died young. While most of Europe followed Germany's lead, the United States, with its tradition of self-reliance, was reluctant to adopt these programs.

After the 1929 stock market crash, America's economy collapsed: banks failed, factories closed, and millions of Americans lost their jobs. During the Great Depression, many suffered serious financial hardship. Older Americans were especially hard-hit. Nancy Altman, who chairs the board of directors of the Pension Rights Center, explains: "Even harder than being unemployed in the midst of the Depression was being unemployed and old. By 1934, over half of the elderly in America were impoverished. If you were old, unable to work, and your children were unable to support you, the poorhouse was generally all that remained between you and life on the street."[2] Some states tried to provide financial aid to older Americans and others in need, but they, too, were strapped for funds and could only help a small percentage of those who needed help.

The New Deal

In 1933, at the low point of the Depression, Franklin D. Roosevelt became president. At the time, a doctor from California, Francis Townsend, proposed that the federal government pay a $200-per-month benefit to every person older than 60, on the condition that the money be spent immediately. Supporters believed that the benefits would reduce poverty among the elderly and at the same time stimulate the economy. Townsend's idea quickly won a following, and Americans urged lawmakers to adopt it. Sensing the nation's mood, Roosevelt asked his cabinet to draw up a social-insurance program that he could propose to Congress. An economist named Abraham Epstein called Roosevelt's program "Social Security," and the phrase caught on with the public.

President Roosevelt envisioned a social insurance program that not only provided pensions to older Americans but health insurance and unemployment benefits as well. He also wanted Social Security to be a permanent government program. Even though Roosevelt was willing to support welfare programs—which provide benefits to those who prove they need help—on a short-term basis, his long-term goal was an insurance program. Insurance spreads the risk of an event, such as a house fire, over a large number of people, minimizing the chances that the event will cause financial ruin to the person who suffers it. Social insurance operates on a similar principle: a large number of individuals contribute to a special fund; and those who suffer some misfortune, such as becoming unemployed, would be paid out of that fund. In order to receive benefits, workers must be insured, a status they achieve by working the requisite amount of time in employment that is covered by Social Security. The concept of "insured status" is fundamental to Social Security. Workers who meet the criteria for insured status receive benefits as the result of an "insured event." When Social Security began, the insured event was aging and retirement. In later years, the list of insured events was expanded to include death and disability.[3]

In 1935, Congress passed the Social Security Act.[4] When Roosevelt signed it on August 14, he told the nation: "We can never insure one hundred percent of the population against one hundred percent of the hazards and vicissitudes of life, but we have tried to frame a law which will give some measure of protection to the average citizen and to his family against the loss of a job and against poverty-ridden old age."[5] Even though "Social Security" is shorthand for retirement benefits, other portions

President Franklin D. Roosevelt signs the Social Security Act of 1935 in the Cabinet Room of the White House in Washington, D.C., as Congress members Robert Doughton, Robert Wagner, John Dingell Sr., an unidentified man, Secretary of Labor Frances Perkins, Pat Harrison, and David Lewis, look on.

of the Social Security Act provided financial aid to a variety of Americans, including unemployed workers, children, and people with disabilities.

The retirement portion of the Social Security Act was structured as follows:

- Employers and workers had to pay a new federal tax, called a "contribution," to fund Social Security.
- The system was "progressive," meaning that low-wage workers received more-generous benefits compared to what they had earned in their working years.

• Because Social Security was an insurance program, coverage was nationwide and, for most workers, mandatory.

One distinctive feature of Social Security was the way in which funds were handled. The intention was to create a "reserve" of workers' contributions, which the government would control until it came time to pay benefits to workers who reached retirement age. Employers' and workers' contributions were placed into what soon became a "trust fund." (Actually, there are two trust funds, one for the Old Age and Survivors Insurance [OASI] program and another for the Disability Insurance [DI] program.) Benefits are paid out of the trust fund rather than the federal government's general revenue, an arrangement that helps prevent Congress from "raiding" Social Security to fund other programs. In 2009, the Social Security Administration (SSA) estimated that the trust funds had a combined balance of $2.56 trillion, and that they took in $136.9 billion more than they paid out in 2009. However, the SSA warns that when the very large "baby boom" generation (those born between 1946 and 1964) retires, Social Security will pay out more in benefits than it takes in. If this trend continues, it would eventually empty the trust funds. There is considerable debate as to whether the trust funds can be put on a more solid financial footing and, if so, what is the best way to accomplish that.

Passage of the Social Security Act did not end the debate. Social Security was an issue in the 1936 presidential campaign. The Republicans argued that the system would go bankrupt, leaving retirees with worthless government IOUs. However, the GOP lost the election. Social Security also had to survive a constitutional challenge. In 1937, the U.S. Supreme Court handed down two decisions, *Charles C. Steward Machine Company v. Davis* and *Helvering v. Davis*, which upheld the constitutionality of the Social Security Act. In the *Davis* decisions, Justice Benjamin Cardozo said that the concept of "the general welfare," an area of federal power spelled out in the Constitution, changes with the times. He concluded that it was appropriate for the federal government to act, saying:

The problem is plainly national in area and dimensions. Moreover, laws of the separate states cannot deal with it effectively. . . . A system of old age pensions has

The Social Security Act of 1935

The Social Security Act was signed into law by President Franklin D. Roosevelt on August 14, 1935. It consisted of a preamble and 11 titles. The preamble stated that the purpose of the act was "to provide for the general welfare," a power of Congress spelled out in the U.S. Constitution. Because the act faced a constitutional challenge, it was divided into titles in order to save those portions that were not found unconstitutional.

Titles II and VIII deal with **old-age benefits**, which most Americans think of when they hear the phrase "Social Security." The definition of "employment" covered most workers except agricultural workers, domestic servants working in someone's home, government employees, and employees of nonprofit organizations. Title II also defined a "qualified individual," who was eligible to receive benefits: a person who was at least 65 years old, had earned at least $2,000 between the end of 1936 and his or her sixty-fifth birthday, and had worked at least one day in five different calendar years.

Title II also directed the Treasury to create an Old-Age Reserve Account. Money in the trust fund had to be invested in interest-bearing government obligations, a requirement that still applies. It directed the Social Security Board, also created by the act, to pay benefits to qualified individuals. The first benefit checks would be issued on January 1, 1942; the maximum benefit would be $85 per month, with no adjustment for inflation. A beneficiary could not transfer his or her right to receive Social Security benefits, and benefits could not be taken away in a lawsuit filed against the beneficiary.

Title VIII established a funding mechanism for old-age compensation. Workers had to pay an income tax on their wages; and employers had to pay an equal amount, called an "excise" tax, on those same wages. The original rate of both taxes was 1 percent of the first $3,000 of wages. That rate has been increased a number of times over the years, and is currently 6.2 percent of the first $106,800 in wages.

Title III dealt with **unemployment insurance**. That title appropriated money to the states to pay unemployment compensation. If the Social Security Board special dangers of its own if put in force in one state and rejected in another. The existence of such a system is a bait to the needy and dependent elsewhere, encouraging

certified that a state had a qualifying unemployment-insurance law, the Treasury was required to pay an amount the board found necessary "for the proper administration" of that law. To qualify, a state unemployment-insurance fund had to meet certain requirements. Benefits had to be paid through state unemployment offices. States were not allowed to deny benefits for any of the following reasons: refusing to work as a strikebreaker; refusing to take a job whose wages, hours, or other working conditions were "substantially less favorable" than those for similar work in the area; or turning down a position that would bar the worker from belonging to a labor union.

Title IX provided that workers covered by Social Security were also covered by federal unemployment insurance. It also required employers of eight or more workers to pay another excise tax to support the unemployment insurance program. However, most of that tax would be refunded to employers located in states with qualifying unemployment-insurance laws.

The Social Security Act also provided for other categories of benefits:

- Title I: aged needy individuals.

- Title IV: children younger than 16 who had been deprived of parental support and were living with relatives. This is now known as the Aid for Families with Dependent Children program.

- Title V: health care for certain children and physically handicapped individuals, especially those living in rural or distressed areas.

- Title VI: public health services.

- Title X: blind needy individuals.

State programs had to meet certain requirements in order to qualify for federal funds. For example, programs had to be administered by a state agency, and a person denied benefits had to be given a fair hearing.

Source: Public Law 74-271 (49 Stat. 620), codified as 42 U.S.C. §§301 and following.

them to migrate and seek a haven of repose. Only a power that is national can serve the interests of all.[6]

Moving Toward Universal Coverage

When he signed the Social Security Act, President Roosevelt referred to it as a "cornerstone" in a structure that was far from complete. In 1939, Congress expanded Social Security for the first time, extending protection to workers' dependents and survivors. It also moved up the date for paying the first retirement benefits from 1942 to 1940 in order to stimulate the economy. Roosevelt continued to push for expansion of the program. In his 1945 budget message to Congress, Roosevelt said:

> From the inception of the social security program in 1935 it has been planned to increase the number of persons covered and to provide protection against hazards not initially included. . . . I recommend an increase in the coverage of old-age and survivors' insurance, addition of permanent and temporary disability payments and hospitalization payments beyond the present benefit programs, and liberalization and expansion beyond the present benefit programs, and liberalization and expansion of unemployment compensation in a uniform national system.[7]

Congress was slow to act. As late as 1949, only 3.5 million Americans, a little more than 2 percent of the population, were receiving Social Security benefits. Workers in many occupations were still not covered, and the average benefit check was much smaller than the average benefit paid by state welfare programs.

The modern era of Social Security began in 1950. That year, Congress raised benefits by 77 percent to account for the inflation that had occurred since the Social Security Act became law. By 1954, it had approved two more increases and

In July 1965, President Lyndon B. Johnson signs the Medicare bill as *(from left to right)* First Lady Lady Bird Johnson, former president Harry S. Truman, and former first lady Bess Truman look on. At the bill-signing ceremony, President Johnson enrolled his predecessor, who had advocated such national health insurance while president, as the first Medicare beneficiary and presented him with the first Medicare card.

tripled the number of people receiving benefits. That trend continued for the next two decades, as Congress periodically increased benefits and expanded the pool of those eligible to collect benefits. In 1965, after years of debate, Congress passed what is commonly known as the Medicare Act.[8] The high-water mark for Social Security came seven years later, when Congress increased benefits by 20 percent and "indexed" future benefits: they would automatically increase each year in an amount equal to the rate of inflation. Social Security was—and still is—immensely popular with Americans, especially those of retirement age. Today, more than 50 million people receive Social Security benefits.

The Medicare Act

Health insurance in the United States dates back to the 1920s. Insurance companies offered policies to employers, which they considered a good risk because workers were young and healthy. Employer-based health insurance became popular during World War II because companies could add it to their workers' benefit package without violating wartime wage controls. Thus millions of Americans became covered by employer-based health insurance.

Many Americans, however, still had no insurance. In 1945, President Harry S. Truman asked Congress to establish a national health insurance program. Opponents called the proposal "socialized medicine," and the proposal died. A less-sweeping plan was proposed: health insurance for Social Security beneficiaries. Supporters argued that the government had to step in and help. The number of Americans age 65 or older was increasing, and the cost of health care was growing faster than their incomes. Older individuals were more susceptible to illness and thus unable to buy insurance because insurers were unwilling to insure them. Many older Americans faced poverty as the result of medical bills.

After years of debate, Congress passed the Social Security Act Amendments of 1965, popularly known as the Medicare Act. The act, which has been substantially amended since then, now consists of the following:

- Medicare Part A (hospital insurance), which helps cover hospital, hospice, and in-home health care for those age 65 and older. Although this coverage is free for Social Security recipients, Medicare does not pay all expenses. The beneficiary must pay $1,068 for the first 60 days in the hospital, and longer stays can cost tens of thousands of dollars.

- Medicare Part B (medical insurance), which helps cover doctors' services, outpatient care, and preventive services for those age 65 or older. This part is optional. Those who choose it must pay a premium

Economic Turmoil and Calls for Reform

During the 1970s, economic problems threatened the stability of the Social Security program. America went into a recession after

---

that ranges from $110.50 to $353.60 per month. Part B has a yearly deductible of $155, as well as a co-pay: Medicare pays 80 percent of services covered by Part B, and the beneficiary must pay the rest.

- Medicare Part C ("Medicare Advantage" plans), which are offered by insurance companies approved by Medicare. These plans, which resemble health maintenance organization plans, include Medicare Parts A and B and frequently offer other services such as hearing and dental coverage.

- Medicare Part D (prescription drug coverage), which is offered by private insurance companies approved by Medicare, helps cover the cost of prescription drugs. This program was added to Medicare in 2003.

- Medicaid, a joint federal and state program that helps pay medical costs for people who have both low income and few assets. Medicaid covers some services that Medicare does not cover.

Medicare is funded in part by payroll taxes, currently 1.45 percent of the worker's wages and a matching contribution of 1.45 percent on the employer's part. (Unlike Social Security, there is no maximum on the wages subject to the Medicare tax.) The rest of Medicare's expenses are paid by beneficiaries or out of general government spending.

Medicare does not pay for long-term care, which means nonmedical care such as help with everyday activities like dressing and bathing. This kind of care often takes place in nursing homes. Medicaid may cover long-term care, but only the very poor are eligible for assistance. Because an extended stay in a nursing home is very expensive, many older Americans buy long-term insurance from private companies.

Source: Public Law 89-97. Among other provisions, it created Titles XVIII and XIX of the Social Security Act (Title 42, Sections 1395 and following, of the United States Code).

the 1973 Arab oil embargo. The weak economy provoked the first serious discussion as to whether the program was financially sustainable. In 1977, Congress was forced to raise payroll taxes and, for the first time, scale back benefits. In the early 1980s, as the nation endured another serious recession, policy makers feared that the Social Security system was about to run out of money. President Ronald Reagan created a National Commission on Social Security Reform to "review relevant analyses of the current and long-term financial condition of the Social Security trust funds; identify problems that may threaten the long-term solvency of such funds; analyze potential solutions to such problems that will both assure the financial integrity of the Social Security System and the provision of appropriate benefits."[9] The commission, headed by Alan Greenspan, recommended a number of changes, including higher payroll taxes and gradually raising the retirement age for some current workers. Congress approved those changes in 1983.

Some reformers believed that the 1983 amendments were a stopgap measure that did not address Social Security's basic flaws. They pointed out that the legislation created unfunded liabilities—future obligations for which the money had not yet been set aside. The problem of unfunded liabilities was growing because the number of future retirees was increasing, retirement benefits had become more generous over the years, and new programs such as Medicare had added to the cost of the system. As a result, Social Security was not taking in enough money to pay the benefits the government had promised. They also warned that once the baby boom generation reached retirement age, the system would come under such financial strain that it would inevitably go bankrupt. Reformers thus concluded that Social Security, in its present form, was unsustainable, and they called for fundamental changes to its structure.

The reform movement gained momentum in 1980 when the Cato Institute, a libertarian advocacy organization, published a book titled *Social Security: The Inherent Contradiction.* Its author, Peter J. Ferrara, called for the abolition of Social Security. He said:

The program is fundamentally coercive, forcing all Americans to participate regardless of their desires. . . . The iniquities and negative economic impacts of the system fall more heavily on some of the most vulnerable groups in society—blacks, the poor, women, the elderly, and the young. The program is financed by a regressive payroll tax that imposes a hardship on the poor. Despite recent tax increases and official assurances, the danger that the system will become bankrupt remains real.[10]

At the time Ferrara published his paper, the model for workplace pensions was beginning to change. Traditional pension plans, which promised workers a fixed amount per month in retirement, were being replaced by "defined contribution" plans in which the worker—and usually, but not always, the employer—contributed a fixed amount. That account would grow over the years and provide the worker with a substantial amount of money in retirement. Ferrara's proposal incorporated this model. He called for replacing Social Security with personal retirement accounts, which workers would own and which would be funded with the taxes currently paid to Social Security. Ferrara argued that personal accounts would provide workers with a better return on their investments, and more income in retirement, than Social Security. He also said that personal accounts had other benefits:

Privatization would also reduce or eliminate the coercion and political instability associated with a government-operated program. It would allow greater diversity because individuals would be able to choose from a wide variety of plans and pick the one best suited to their needs. The forces of competition might lead to the development of new and superior plans.[11]

In the years that followed, Ferrara's idea became more popular. Many commentators, and some government officials, lent their support to making personal accounts part of the Social Security system. In 2000, when he was running for president, George W. Bush argued that workers should be allowed to invest some of their payroll taxes in personal accounts. Once

Important Dates in Social Security History

1933—President Franklin D. Roosevelt creates the Committee on Economic Security, which makes recommendations regarding what would become Social Security.

1935—Congress passes the Social Security Act and President Roosevelt signs it into law. The act not only establishes a system of retirement benefits, but also creates the modern system of unemployment insurance and provides welfare benefits for families with children.

1937—The U.S. Supreme Court hands down two opinions, *Charles C. Steward Machine Company v. Davis* and *Helvering v. Davis*, which uphold the constitutionality of the Social Security Act.

1939—Congress amends the Social Security Act to extend protection to dependents and survivors. It also moves up the date for the first retirement benefits from 1942 to 1940, and establishes a Social Security Trust Fund that is separate from the federal budget.

1950—Congress extends Social Security coverage to millions of previously uncovered employees, and increases benefits to account for inflation that occurred since the system was created.

1956—Congress adds disability insurance to Social Security, and allows women to retire at age 62. Five years later, men are also given the option of retiring at age 62.

1965—Congress passes the Medicare Act, which helps pay the hospitalization expenses and doctor bills for those age 65 or older. The act also creates Medicaid, which helps pay medical expenses of poorer Americans.

1968–1985—Surpluses in the Social Security system are included as part of the federal government's overall finances. Critics argue that the so-called "unified budget" makes deficits and the national debt look smaller than they really are.

he was in the White House, he created the Commission to Strengthen Social Security. The commission's report, released in December 2001, offered three alternatives, each of which called for such accounts.

1972—Congress approves a one-time 20-percent increase in benefits, along with automatic annual increases tied to the cost of living starting in 1975. It also combines several federally funded programs into the Supplementary Security Income (SSI) program, a welfare program based on need.

1977—A serious recession forces Congress to scale back Social Security for the first time. Payroll taxes are raised, and the formula for determining the amount of benefits is changed.

1980—The first 401(k) accounts are offered by employers. These plans allow workers to set aside part of their income into an account that can grow, tax free, until retirement. Many employers contribute to 401(k) plans as part of their workers' package of benefits.

1981—Another serious recession leaves the Social Security system in danger of being unable to pay benefits. President Reagan creates the National Commission on Social Security, headed by Alan Greenspan. The Greenspan Commission recommends keeping Social Security's structure intact, but shoring up its finances by raising the retirement age and increasing payroll taxes. Congress makes those changes in 1983.

1997—The Advisory Council on Social Security recommends that the Social Security Trust Fund divert some of its money from Treasury bonds to corporate stocks and bonds. Some members of the council also recommend making personal retirement accounts part of Social Security.

2003—Congress passes Medicare Part D, the prescription drug benefit for older Americans. It is the largest expansion of Social Security since 1965.

2009—Nearly 51 million Americans, or about one in six, are receiving Social Security benefits.

According to the latest projection, the Social Security system will begin to run annual deficits by 2015. Those deficits will exhaust Social Security's old age trust fund by 2037.

After President Bush was reelected, he made Social Security reform the central focus of his second-term agenda. In his 2005 State of the Union address, Bush warned members of Congress: "One of America's most important institutions . . . is also in need of wise and effective reform. Social Security was a great moral success of the 20th century, and we must honor its great purposes in this new century. The system, however, on its current path, is headed toward bankruptcy."[12] He urged lawmakers to make personal accounts part of the reformed Social Security system.

The president's plan encountered strong opposition, especially from retiree groups and liberal organizations. As a result, Congress decided not to change Social Security's basic structure. Nevertheless, advocates of reform contend that the economic recession that began in late 2007, which included a wave of corporate bankruptcies and a steep drop in housing prices and the stock market, make it all the more important that we take steps to repair Social Security's finances. Reformers also warn that with a huge generation about to retire, we must act now.

Summary

Retirement did not become commonplace until the last century. Before that, many spent their final years in poverty. The Social Security Act, passed by Congress in 1935, helps protect older Americans from falling into poverty. Although Social Security started modestly, it has grown significantly and now provides benefits to tens of millions of Americans. Reformers warn that Social Security will not have enough money to pay the benefits promised to future retirees. To make up the shortfall, they propose giving workers the option to invest part of their wages into personal accounts instead of a government-run fund. Supporters, however, insist that Social Security is financially sound and that its basic structure does not need major changes.

Social Security Is Unsustainable

In 1936, at a campaign appearance in Milwaukee, Wisconsin, Republican presidential candidate Alf Landon warned the audience about Social Security:

> The worker's cash comes into the Treasury. What is done with it? The law requires the Treasury to buy Government bonds. What happens when the Treasury buys Government bonds? Well, at present, when there is a deficit, the Treasury gives some nice new bonds in exchange for the cash which the Treasury gives the Treasury. Now, what happens to the cash that the Treasury gives the Treasury? The answer is painfully simple. We have good spenders in Washington, as they spend the cash the Treasury gives the Treasury. . . . The

workers asked for a pension and all they have received
is another tax.[1]

Reformers believe that Landon was right. They argue that
Congress has spent workers' Social Security taxes on federal
programs and has left future retirees with IOUs. The reformers
argue that unless Congress overhauls Social Security, the government will eventually be forced to borrow more money, raise
taxes, or cut benefits to retirees. Any of these actions would have
unpleasant consequences for many Americans.

Population patterns have changed since 1935.

America's population is vastly different now from what it was
when the Social Security Act became law. Someone born in 1935
could expect to live 61.7 years, so it was more likely than not that
he or she would die before reaching retirement age. By 2005,
average life expectancy had risen to 77.8 years, a figure that is
expected to rise in future years. Longer life spans have resulted
in a steep rise in the number of older Americans. When the
Industrial Revolution began in the mid-eighteenth century, only
2 to 3 percent of the population was 65 years old or older. Today,
that age group accounts for 12 percent, and, by 2040, their share
of the population is expected to be 20 percent or more.

The population of retirees is already large, and will grow
even more as the baby boomers reach retirement age. In fact,
the oldest members of that generation are already eligible for
benefits. In 2011, they will become eligible for Medicare. Not
only is the number of retirees growing but they are also spending more years in retirement. That has been happening for
decades. In 1965, the typical male worker left the labor force
at approximately age 66, and could expect to live 13 years in
retirement. By 2003, the typical male worker retired at age
63, and could expect to live almost 19 years in retirement.
Furthermore, today's retirement-age Americans are healthier

than those of the 1930s. Technology has eliminated many of the dangerous and physically demanding jobs, and advances in medicine allow older people to stay active longer. Some reformers argue the retirement age should be "indexed" to account for longer lives, in which case it would be somewhere between age 70 and age 75.

The problem of the baby boomers' retirement is made worse by a steep drop in the number of children born after the baby boom ended. In 1957, the nation's birth rate peaked at 3.68 children per woman. Shortly thereafter, the birth rate steadily fell. During the 1970s and 1980s, it fell below 2.1 children per woman, the minimum needed to avoid a loss of population. Even though the birth rate has risen somewhat since then, it remains well below baby boom levels. Changes in the birth rate, combined with longer time spent in retirement, mean that a shrinking number of workers will be called on to support a growing number of retirees. In his 2005 State of the Union address, President Bush explained the problem:

> Social Security was created decades ago, for a very different era. In those days people did not live as long, benefits were much lower than they are today, and a half century ago, about 16 workers paid into the system for each person drawing benefits. Our society has changed in ways the founders of Social Security could not have foreseen. In today's world, people are living longer and therefore drawing benefits longer—and those benefits are scheduled to rise dramatically over the next few decades. And instead of 16 workers paying in for every beneficiary, right now it's only about three workers— and over the next few decades, that number will fall to just two workers per beneficiary. With each passing year, fewer workers are paying ever-higher benefits to an ever-larger number of retirees.[2]

Social Security's costs are growing rapidly.
Social Security is an entitlement program that guarantees benefits to everyone who meets the requirements established by

Definitions Pertaining to Social Security

Actuarial balance. Equality between the Social Security system's future revenues and future costs. As of 2010, the system is 2 percent out of actuarial balance, which means that a payroll tax increase of 2 percent, or benefit cuts equal to that amount, are needed to keep revenue in line with benefits.

Consumer Price Index (CPI). A tool used to measure inflation. The CPI, which is compiled by the Department of Labor, represents the price of a "basket" of products and services such as food, housing, and transportation.

Defined-benefit plan. The "traditional" pension plan under which an employer contributes money for its workers' retirement. A worker who meets certain criteria—generally, age and years on the job—can draw a fixed monthly pension, the size of which depends on how much he or she earned while working. Social Security is based on the defined-benefit model.

Defined-contribution plan. A plan under which an employee contributes part of his or her wages to an account, where the balance grows until the employee retires. The employee owns the money in the account and is responsible for investing it. Personal accounts, which reformers favor, are based on the defined-contribution model.

Entitlement program. A government program that guarantees benefits to those who meet the requirements established by law. Social Security and Medicare are two of the best-known entitlement programs; others include farm price supports and unemployment benefits.

Federal Insurance Contributions Act (FICA). A payroll tax system under which workers contribute 6.2 percent of their wages to the Social Security trust funds, and employers pays a tax equal to 6.2 percent of their workers' wages.

"Pay as you go." A term used to describe Social Security's finances. Payments to current beneficiaries are made from current revenues, which largely come from payroll taxes. The opposite of a "pay as you go" retirement system is *pre-funded*, which means contributions accumulate in an account over time and are paid out when the beneficiary reaches retirement age.

law. For more than a generation, however, the Social Security system has failed to take in enough money to pay those benefits in full. According to the Social Security Administration,

Social insurance. A program that requires everyone to belong to a system that protects them against various economic risks, such as old age, unemployment, or disability. Most social insurance programs require those who earn money to pay into a government-run system, which, in turn, pays benefits to those who qualify for them.

Social Security Administration (SSA). An independent federal agency that administers the Social Security system. It is headed by a commissioner who is appointed by the president.

Subsidy. A government policy that provides a financial reward for an activity considered useful to society, such as giving to charity or owning a home. The federal government subsidizes employer-sponsored retirement plans by allowing an employer to deduct contributions to those plans from its federal income tax bill.

Supplemental Security Income (SSI). A program, which is part of Social Security, that provides cash to needy and disabled Americans to pay for life's necessities. Unlike Social Security, SSI is a welfare program based on need and is funded out of the federal government's general tax revenues.

Tax credit. A reduction in an individual's tax bill on account of having done something the government wants to encourage. Some tax credits are *refundable*, meaning that if the credit reduces a person's tax liability below zero, the person will receive a check for the difference from the government. Many Social Security reform plans include refundable tax credits, which would provide low-income workers with cash to invest in personal retirement accounts.

Trust fund. A fund created by Congress to hold Social Security payroll taxes that have not yet been spent on benefits. Actually, there are two Social Security trust funds: the Old-Age and Survivors Insurance (OASI) trust fund and the smaller Disability Insurance (DI) trust fund. Trust fund assets must be invested in a special series of interest-earning U.S. Treasury bonds.

Welfare. A government program that provides money or services to people who are poor or who face an emergency. Welfare benefits are provided on the basis of need and are not, like Social Security, a form of insurance.

the system faces a shortfall of 2 percent of taxable payroll over the next 75 years. In other words, payroll taxes must be raised 2 percent, or cuts of the same size must be made to retirees' benefits, to ensure the system's long-term survival. It has been estimated that Social Security has unfunded liabilities of $15.5 trillion. That amount is larger than the nation's Gross Domestic Product (GDP)—the total value of goods and services produced in one year. A private corporation with unfunded liabilities of this size would be a candidate for bankruptcy—a legal proceeding in which the corporation's creditors are given only a fraction of what they are owed. Reformers warn that the government's creditors, including future retirees, could be similarly shortchanged in the future.

In 2009, the SSA estimated that the trust funds collected $819.4 billion, most of that in payroll taxes, and paid out $682.5 billion, for a surplus of $136.9 billion. Those figures, however, create a misleading impression. That same year, the SSA warned: "Social Security is not sustainable over the long term at current benefit and tax rates. Within 7 years the program will begin paying more in benefits than it collects in taxes. . . . By 2037 the trust funds will be exhausted. At that point, payroll taxes and other income will flow into the fund but will be sufficient to pay only 76% of program costs."[3] Medicare's finances are even shakier. The trustees of the Social Security system project that the Hospital Insurance (HI) Trust Fund, which pays Medicare Part A benefits, will run out of money in 2029.

Since 2009, Social Security's financial picture has grown substantially worse. The recession that began in late 2007 eliminated an estimated eight million jobs and caused a sharp increase in the number of workers who opted to retire early and collect benefits because they could not find a job. This combination of lower payroll tax revenue and higher benefit payments has strained the Social Security system. In March 2010, the nonpartisan Congressional Budget Office projected that the system would run a $29 billion deficit in fiscal year 2010 and would

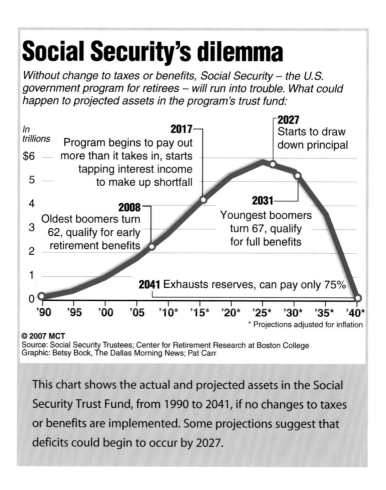

Social Security's dilemma

Without change to taxes or benefits, Social Security – the U.S. government program for retirees – will run into trouble. What could happen to projected assets in the program's trust fund:

In trillions

2017 — Program begins to pay out more than it takes in, starts tapping interest income to make up shortfall

2027 Starts to draw down principal

2008 — Oldest boomers turn 62, qualify for early retirement benefits

2031 — Youngest boomers turn 67, qualify for full benefits

2041 Exhausts reserves, can pay only 75%

'90 '95 '00 '05 '10* '15* '20* '25* '30* '35* '40*

* Projections adjusted for inflation

© 2007 MCT
Source: Social Security Trustees; Center for Retirement Research at Boston College
Graphic: Betsy Bock, The Dallas Morning News; Pat Carr

This chart shows the actual and projected assets in the Social Security Trust Fund, from 1990 to 2041, if no changes to taxes or benefits are implemented. Some projections suggest that deficits could begin to occur by 2027.

continue to pay out more in benefits than it received in taxes in fiscal years 2011 through 2013.

Entitlement programs have a huge impact on the nation's economy. Niall Ferguson, a professor at Harvard University, explains:

> Today the average retiree receives Social Security, Medicare and Medicaid benefits totaling $21,000 a year. Multiply this by the current 36 million elderly and you see why these programmes already consume such a

large proportion of federal tax revenues. And that proportion is bound to rise, not only because the number of retirees is going up but also because the cost of benefits like Medicare are out of control, rising at double the rate of inflation. The 2003 extension of Medicare to cover prescription drugs only made matters worse.[4]

Experts have known about this problem for years. In 1994, a bipartisan commission warned: "In 2030, unless appropriate policy changes are made in the interim, projected spending for Medicare, Medicaid, Social Security, and Federal employee retirement programs alone will consume all tax revenues collected by the federal government."[5] Government agencies agree that the growth of entitlement programs represents a budgetary time bomb. Congress, however, has ignored these warnings. Instead of scaling back entitlements, it has added to them. Most recently, it added a prescription drug benefit to Medicare. According to a 2008 estimate by the Centers for Medicare and Medicaid Services, that program alone will cost $395 million over the next decade.

Half-hearted reform measures have not worked.
Reformers contend that tax increases without change to Social Security's basic structure only postpones the inevitable. In 1977, Congress raised payroll taxes and, for the first time ever, scaled back benefits. At the time, policy makers claimed the amendments gave Social Security an extra 50 years of life. Just a few years later, the system again faced the possibility that it could not pay benefits. That crisis led to the Greenspan Commission reforms, passed by Congress in 1983. Again, policy makers claimed that the reforms would ensure the system's long-term survival.

By 2001, however, the system was again out of balance. The President's Commission to Strengthen Social Security reported that "under current law Social Security's burden on future taxpayers is projected to rise quickly during the next thirty years, from its current level of 10.5 percent of taxable payroll to over 17 percent of taxable payroll by 2030. Thereafter, the burden continues to grow, albeit at a somewhat slower pace. By 2075, the burden will exceed 19 percent of taxable payroll."[6] When the next crisis inevitably arrives, the response will be another round of half-hearted measures—most likely another increase in the payroll tax.

Reformers also believe that the growth of Social Security, combined with its heavy reliance on the payroll tax, has harmed the economy. In 1980, Peter J. Ferrara wrote:

> The social security program has several important negative effects on the American economy. It causes severe losses in savings and capital investment, a reduction of national income and economic growth, and decreased employment. With the tremendous growth in the size of the program in recent years, these negative impacts have become too powerful and too serious to be ignored.[7]

Nevertheless, three years after he made that statement, Congress raised payroll taxes again.

We must act now.

Over the next generation, the population of older Americans will practically double, putting added strain on Social Security. With that in mind, reformers warn that we have little time to make changes that will ensure the system's long-term survival. In 2001, the Commission to Strengthen Social Security warned that a final window of opportunity was about to close:

> For the past 20 years, Social Security surpluses have been used primarily to fund other government spending. If, instead, these surpluses are put into personal accounts, they are more likely to be used for their

intended purpose of funding future Social Security benefits. According to Intermediate projections of the Social Security Trustees, Social Security is expected to run cash surpluses totaling $811 billion in present value between now and 2016. The Commission believes that these resources should be used to fund the transition to personal accounts, rather than to finance other government spending programs.[8]

"The Inherent Contradiction"

Peter J. Ferrara first made the case for personal retirement accounts in his 1980 book *Social Security: The Inherent Contradiction*. According to Ferrara, Social Security's "inherent contradiction" is that it was designed to be both an insurance program and a welfare program. The result was a system with the worst features of both.

In Ferrara's view, Social Security was on a self-destructive course from the outset because Congress paid more in benefits to the first generation of retirees than those retirees contributed to the system. After the first generation retired, Social Security had huge benefit obligations the second generation had to meet. Members of the second generation, who had paid into the system, believed that they were entitled to benefits when they reached retirement age. Their retirement, however, burdened the system with unfunded liabilities—it owed more in benefits than it could collect in payroll taxes—which meant that taxes had to be raised in order to pay for those benefits.

Ferrara argued that the cycle could not go on indefinitely. At some point, tax increases would run into political resistance, and people would question the system's financial soundness. By 1980, when he published his book, some experts were raising those concerns. In Ferrara's opinion, the Social Security system was a drag on the economy because it was financed by a payroll tax that reduced savings and investment. That tax was regressive—that is, it took a higher percentage of poor workers' wages, hurting the very people a welfare program was supposed to help. Social Security was also a bad investment because workers could receive a higher rate of return by investing their payroll taxes in accounts that they owned.

Even after the commission released its report, Congress failed to enact Social Security reform. In his 2005 State of the Union Address, President Bush reminded lawmakers how urgent the situation had become. He told them:

I recognize that 2018 and 2042 may seem like a long way off. But those dates are not so distant, as any parent will tell you. If you have a 5-year-old, you're already

The poor were not the only victims of Social Security. Ferrara contended that the system also shortchanged minorities, who typically earned less and lived shorter lives and thus received less in benefits. In addition, he accused Social Security of being unfair to nontraditional women because it still expected women to stay home and be wives and mothers.

Ferrara opposed Social Security on philosophical grounds as well, as it was not a voluntary system. Because Social Security taxes future generations that never had an opportunity to object to being in the system, he called it a classic case of "taxation without representation."

Finally, Ferrara accused the government of lying about Social Security, for instance, by using the word *insurance* to describe future benefits for which no money had been set aside. He also maintained that the Social Security trust fund was a sham because the money in it was immediately paid to current retirees rather than invested to pay for future retirees.

Ferrara's proposal was a radical one. His "ideal system" would result in the outright abolition of Social Security. Welfare-like aspects of Social Security—such as benefits for spouses and dependents, who have not necessarily paid into the system—would be transferred from Social Security to a different federal program or, perhaps, private charity. More important, Social Security itself would be replaced with a system of private accounts. Ferrara pointed out that private companies offered the same benefits as Social Security at a lower price. If payroll taxes were abolished, workers could invest most of that money in a personal retirement account; and they could also spend the rest of it to buy life and disability insurance, if they thought it necessary. Ferrara even believed that Medicare could be replaced by a system under which workers paid premiums early in their career for insurance that would cover their medical expenses after they retired.

concerned about how you'll pay for college tuition 13 years down the road. If you've got children in their 20s, as some of us do, the idea of Social Security collapsing before they retire does not seem like a small matter. And it should not be a small matter to the United States Congress.[9]

As it turned out, the dates cited by the president were optimistic. Even if Congress acts today, Social Security reform will take years to implement. Changes to the system will affect tens of millions of people, who need time to make alternate plans for their retirement. Peter Diamond and Peter Orszag explain:

> Think of Social Security as a giant supertanker. Just as it takes time to change the course of a supertanker, so, too, changing the course of Social Security must be done gradually over time, to allow the millions of people whose lives are affected by Social Security to make the proper adjustments to their retirement planning. So, even though the problem may seem far away, it makes sense to begin addressing it soon.[10]

It is already too late to change current retirees' benefits without causing financial hardship. According to the Social Security Administration, those benefits are the "major source"—more than half—of income for 52 percent of married couples older than 65 and for 72 percent of unmarried individuals older than 65. Likewise, "near-retirees," generally defined as those older than 55, have little time to make alternate plans. For that reason, the reform plans spelled out by the Commission to Strengthen Social Security would keep the traditional system intact for both retirees and near-retirees.

Unless Social Security and other entitlement programs are reined in soon, the country faces serious economic consequences.

During the past 25 years, America has spent much more than it has collected in revenue. Years of deficit spending made the United States the world's number-one debtor nation. According to USDebtClock.org, the national debt was more than $13.8 trillion at the end of 2010 and is growing quickly. Worse yet, as of February 2010, America's two biggest creditors were Japan ($768.8 billion) and China ($755.4 billion). Foreign-held debt endangers our national security. Menzie Chinn, a professor at the University of Wisconsin, warns that the government must get its financial house in order:

> Taking the initiative now to reduce borrowing will give the United States greater control over its economic destiny. Failure to do so will cede to foreign governments increasing influence over the nation's fate. Perhaps equally alarming, it will lead to slower growth, escalating trade friction, and reduced American influence in political and economic spheres.[11]

Summary

Social Security was sustainable during its early years because a large population of working Americans was supporting a small number of retirees. That is no longer the case. Benefits have become more generous, and more people are eligible to collect them. High birth rates after World War II created the huge baby boom generation, which is reaching retirement age. They will live longer and spend more time in retirement than previous generations. As a result, Social Security will eventually run out of money. Congress has raised payroll taxes numerous times, but the system's long-term problems continue. Reformers warn that without fundamental change, Social Security cannot pay promised benefits to retirees. They also warn that failure to control entitlement program costs will have disastrous effects on the nation's economy.

Social Security Is a Wise Investment

Social Security is one of America's most successful government programs. Even President George W. Bush, who argued for Social Security reform, praised it as an important American institution and one of the most successful programs of the twentieth century. The Social Security Administration (SSA) is a highly respected federal agency. In her book *The Battle for Social Security*, Nancy Altman describes how SSA employees worked overtime to get benefit checks to the families of those killed in the September 11, 2001, terrorist attacks:

> Today, virtually all working Americans continue to contribute to the 9/11 families every payday. The money withheld from every worker's paycheck goes into the program's Old Age and Survivors Insurance Trust Fund, out of which those victims' families receive benefits.

Virtually every child who lost a parent in the terrorist attack will receive a Social Security check every month until his or her late teens. So will the children's surviving parents who care for them.[1]

Social Security is a successful program.

The design of Social Security was ingenious. President Roosevelt insisted that the program be funded through payroll taxes rather than through the general government budget. He also wanted the system to be self-sufficient. The President's Commission to Strengthen Social Security explains:

> Social Security's self-financing design is an important component of its policy basis and its political support. Self-financing helps to ensure fiscal discipline, by assuring that the program's benefits and dedicated revenues remain aligned. Social Security's separate accounting is also an important protection for the program, helping to ensure that all of its dedicated revenues are ultimately used to pay Social Security benefits.[2]

When Social Security was created during the Great Depression, millions of Americans found themselves in poverty through no fault of their own. Even though they were unable to contribute to the system, they received benefits anyway. Economists Peter Diamond and Peter Orszag applaud that decision:

> The decision, made early in the history of Social Security, to provide the first generations of beneficiaries benefits disproportionate to their contributions represented sound policy. It was a humane response to the suffering imposed by World War I, the Great Depression, and World War II on Americans who came of age during those years, and it helped to reduce

This poster issued in 1935 by the Social Security Board urged citizens to take advantage of the recently passed Social Security Act. Since its inception, Social Security has been an important part of preventing older Americans from sliding into poverty.

unacceptably high rates of poverty among them in old age. Moreover, the higher benefits not only helped the recipients themselves but also relieved part of the burden on their families and friends, and on the taxpayers of that era, who would otherwise have contributed more to their support. Benefits paid by Social Security reduced the cost of transfers to the elderly poor from other programs and reduced the need for children to provide financial and other support to their parents.[3]

Benefit payments to that first generation of retirees created a "legacy debt" in the form of obligations to future retirees. Eliminating that debt would create an even worse problem: it would require some future generation to pay for their own retirement on top of their parents' generation's retirement. Social Security's structure avoids that problem by creating what is known as a "contract between the generations," an ongoing system in which younger Americans finance older Americans' retirement in return for the expectation that their own retirement will be financed by generations to come.

Social Security reflects American values.

President Roosevelt intended that Social Security be an insurance program, not a welfare program. Nancy Altman, who also heads the Center for Pension Rights, points out that welfare programs are designed for people who are already poor, while social insurance programs prevent workers from becoming poor in the first place. She also says that welfare penalizes savers and workers by stripping them of eligibility for benefits, while insurance encourages people to keep earning and saving. Altman adds: "Social Security was created with basic American values in mind. . . . It was built on the premise of work. Only those who have worked long enough to gain insured status and those workers' dependents are eligible for benefits."[4] She adds that Social

Security is conservatively managed. By law, the money in the trust funds must be invested in U.S. Treasury bonds, which are more reliable than other paper investments. Furthermore, public officials who are legally obligated to act on behalf of beneficiaries and no one else manage the trust funds.

The progressive nature of Social Security helps those with low incomes. The formula for calculating benefits gives the most weight to the first dollars earned during one's career, and also provides a minimum benefit to workers who qualify. Low wage earners receive a higher percentage of their working income in retirement than high-wage earners, giving them

How Social Security Benefits Are Calculated

The Social Security Act's retirement benefit structure is designed to be "progressive," meaning that the system replaces more of a low-earning worker's income in retirement than it does for a high-earning worker.

To determine the worker's Average Indexed Monthly Earnings (AIME), the SSA assembles the worker's record of "covered" employment—whenever he or she paid taxes to Social Security. The highest-earning 35 years are counted; if the worker's career was shorter than 35 years, the other years are given a value of zero. After all earnings are assembled, the next step is to index them. Wages for most of the worker's career are increased to reflect the amount by which wages had risen nationwide. Next, the worker's indexed earnings are added up and then divided by 420, the number of months in 35 years. That amount is the worker's AIME.

After AIME is determined, the next step is to compute the Primary Insurance Amount (PIA), which is the monthly amount the worker would earn if he or she retires at the "full retirement age." (Depending on when the worker was born, full retirement age is somewhere between 65 and 67.) For workers who first became eligible in 2009, the PIA was determined using the following formula:

added protection against falling into poverty in retirement. Social Security also stimulates the economy. It allows older workers to leave the workforce, freeing up jobs for younger workers. In addition, benefits are "counter cyclical," which means that they enable people to keep spending money during recessions when businesses face the greatest risk of closing due to a lack of customers. It has been estimated that pension income accounts for 10 percent of all consumer spending. Social Security will take on even greater importance in the future, as fewer retirees will receive traditional company pensions. Fast-growing industries such as service and retail are

- 90 percent of AIME, up to $744;

- 32 percent on the amount above $744 up to $4,483; and

- 15 percent on the amount above $4,483.

There is a maximum allowable benefit, which depends on the age at which a worker retires. In 2009, the maximum for a person who retired at age 66, the full retirement age, was $2,323 per month.

If a worker opts to retire before reaching full retirement age, his or her benefits are reduced. The reduction for a person who retires at age 62, the earliest age allowable, is 25 percent. Conversely, a person who puts off retirement until after reaching full retirement age is given "delayed retirement credits," which result in higher benefit payments. These differences in benefits are intended to achieve "actuarial fairness," meaning that retirees receive approximately the same total amount of benefits regardless of when they retire.

The final step is the indexing of benefits to offset the effects of inflation. The U.S. Department of Labor determines the Consumer Price Index (CPI), which represents the average price of a "basket" of consumer goods and services. By law, retirees' benefits automatically increase once a year by the amount the CPI has risen. In both 2009 and 2010, there was no increase in the CPI, and thus, benefit levels did not change.

least likely to offer pensions, while those industries that tra-
ditionally offered them—such as the auto, steel, and telecom-
munications industries—are shrinking.

Social Security also makes "near-retirees," those between
ages 55 and 65, more secure. Dean Baker, the co-director of the
Center for Economic and Policy Research, argues that near-
retirees are more likely to support the economy today if they
know they will receive Social Security benefits after they retire.
Baker adds that the government has resorted to stimulus measures in the past:

> Thinking people who care about future generations
> should be insisting that the government spend whatever
> is necessary to get the economy back on its feet, just as
> we spent as much as was necessary to win World War II.
> There is no serious prospect that we will face the same
> debt burden as we did after World War II, which hap-
> pened to precede the most prosperous three decades in
> U.S. history.[5]

Reformers exaggerate Social Security's flaws.

Reformers often contend that Social Security is headed for
bankruptcy. That claim is not accurate. The system's trustees
point out that funds have been collecting more in revenue than
pay out in benefits and will have a substantial balance. Even
after the trust funds start running deficits, they will have enough
money to pay promised benefits until 2037. Furthermore, even
after the trust funds are exhausted in 2037, benefits will not fall
to zero. The government will continue collecting payroll taxes,
which are expected to cover 76 percent of benefits. Finally, the
United States will not go bankrupt in the same way as companies like Enron Corporation, the once-huge energy trading
company that nowadays barely exists. Nancy Altman explains:
"Bankruptcy is a meaningless concept when applied to the federal government as a whole or any of its programs. As long as

the federal government has, under the Constitution, 'Power To lay and collect Taxes' and the authority to issue and sell Treasury bonds, it and its programs will not go bankrupt."[6]

For years, critics have called the Social Security system's assets worthless IOUs. President Bush himself made that claim when he campaigned for reform in 2005. That is simply not true. Economists Peter Diamond and Peter Orszag reply:

> The answer . . . is unambiguous: the bonds held by the trust fund are an asset to the Social Security system because they earn interest income and, when the time comes, can be redeemed to pay benefits. The fact that these bonds are "paper" assets does not in any way reduce their value. *All* pension funds hold paper IOUs. . . . The bonds held by the trust fund are, if anything, more secure than other paper assets, given their U.S. government backing.[7]

Nancy Altman adds that critics are wrong when they contend that the trust fund amounts to the government merely "lending money to itself." She likens the Social Security trust fund to a trust created by parents for their children's college education. That trust fund has a separate legal existence, and courts will protect the children's right to the money put into it.

Nor does Social Security's shortfall amount to a "crisis" that requires immediate action. Dean Baker remarks: "[I]t is worth noting other issues that the country will have to deal with in the next 47 years, which are receiving less attention than the projected Social Security shortfall. Those who argue that it is important to address the projected Social Security shortfall now must implicitly believe that this shortfall is more pressing than these other issues that are being largely neglected."[8] Baker identified a number of problems more pressing than Social Security: global warming, the rise of India and China as economic and military powers, and the explosive growth in health care spending.

Social Security does not need restructuring.
Currently, the system's unfunded liabilities are less than 1 percent of GDP. By contrast, the tax cuts passed by Congress in 2001

QUOTABLE

Dean Baker, Co-Director of the Center for Economic and Policy Research

Dean Baker, the co-director of the Center for Economic and Policy Research, does not believe that Social Security's basic structure needs to be overhauled. In a paper published in 2005, he argued that the nation faces more pressing problems, including these:

1. **Excess health care spending will cost $25.2 trillion.** Baker says that by the mid-twenty-first century, health care spending will increase by almost $5,000 a person.

2. **Excess prescription drug spending will cost $5.9 trillion.** Prescription drugs are the fastest-growing component of health care costs, which themselves are increasing faster than the rate of inflation.

3. **The housing bubble will burst, destroying $5.2 trillion in housing wealth.** Just a few years after Baker made this prediction in 2005, the price of both homes and stocks fell sharply, wiping out trillions of dollars in wealth.

4. **The value of the dollar will fall by approximately 30 percent.** Baker said that the dollar was overvalued, and warned that its decline would raise the price of imports and make inflation worse.

5. **The number of people in prison will increase to almost 7 million.** By mid-century, spending on the criminal justice system will grow by another 3.1 percentage points of GDP, or about $1,000 per person.

6. **China's economy will grow to be more than twice the size of the U.S. economy.** The Chinese economy is believed to be more than two-thirds of the size of the U.S. economy and is growing more rapidly than ours. A Central

created an unfunded liability more than twice that size. Experts have offered a number of reform proposals that would keep the system's basic structure intact. Those proposals include:

Intelligence Agency study found that if China continues to spend the same share of its GDP on defense, its military budget would be between five and seven times ours. That, in turn, would mean that the United States would no longer be the world's dominant military power.

7. **India's economy will grow to be more than 60 percent larger than the size of the U.S. economy.** Even though India's economy is now only one-third of the size of the U.S. economy, it is growing so fast that by 2038 it will be larger than ours.

8. **Tens of thousands of animal and plant species will become extinct.** Pollution, the introduction of foreign species to new habitats, the loss of habitat, and the presence of human beings will cause thousands of species to go extinct every year.

9. **The earth's average surface temperature will increase by 1 to 4 degrees Fahrenheit.** Global warming will cause a rise in ocean levels that will trigger flooding in many parts of the world; the migration of species to cooler climates, which would threaten the species that are already there; and a greater likelihood of extreme weather, including droughts, floods, and severe storms.

Baker concludes: "While the politicians who have chosen to focus attention on the projected Social Security shortfall presumably consider it a larger problem than the prospect of spending an additional $25 trillion on health care costs, losing $5 trillion in housing bubble wealth, or seeing the earth's climate seriously disrupted, it is possible that other people would have different priorities. It is important that the public be aware of the other long-term problems facing the country so that it can set its own priorities."*

* Dean Baker, *Things That Will Happen Before Social Security Faces a Shortfall*. Washington, D.C.: Center for Economic and Policy Research, 2005. http://www.policyarchive.org/handle/10207/bitstreams/20738.pdf.

- Taxing all wages, instead of only the first $106,800. Eliminating this wage ceiling would force the highest-earning Americans, who are likely to have substantial retirement savings outside of Social Security, to pay their fair share. Robert Reich, a former secretary of labor, believes this reform alone would go a long way toward closing the gap between revenue and obligations to future retirees.

- Increasing payroll taxes. A modest 1-percent increase would by itself eliminate half of the system's projected shortfall over the next 75 years.

- Reinstating the federal estate tax and putting the revenue into the Social Security trust fund. This tax, which is imposed on a deceased person's assets before family members inherit them, applies only to the richest American families. In 2009, only estates of $3.5 million or more were subject to the tax.

- Allowing the Social Security trustees to invest some trust fund assets in stocks and corporate bonds. Doing so would likely result in higher returns on investment. Nancy Altman believes that the Treasury bonds-only restriction, which dates back to 1935, is obsolete: "Almost all public and private pension funds invest in both stocks and bonds. Public funds that invest in the stock market include the Federal Railroad Retirement Plan, the Federal Reserve Board pension plan, and the plan covering the Tennessee Valley Authority employees."[9]

Although defenders of the current system oppose starving Social Security by diverting payroll taxes into personal retirement accounts, they support "add-on" accounts: a worker's contribution to a personal account would be in addition to his or her Social Security payroll taxes. The government would match the worker's contribution, and even make the contribution on behalf of lower-earning workers. At retirement, the worker would receive two checks, one from the add-on account and one from traditional

Social Security. Today, Social Security replaces 35 percent to 40 percent of the average worker's income. Supporters believe that a system of add-on accounts would leave workers with an even higher percentage of income in retirement.

Social Security offers protection private companies cannot offer.

Social Security offers retirees and their families protection that corporate pension plans and private insurance do not provide. Nancy Altman explains:

> The program protects benefits completely against inflation, whether inflation is slow or galloping. Workers' spouses and former spouses are protected whether a worker has been married to one spouse for life or has been married and divorced multiple times, and the children are protected, like spouses, with supplemental benefits. Those supplemental benefits are in addition to those received by workers and in no way reduce the size of the benefits workers earn for themselves. Moreover, all Americans are benefitted by living in a society where senior citizens have independent sources of income and are not dependent on adult children or welfare. And finally, Social Security has historically provided the security and peace of mind of benefits guaranteed by the United States of America.[10]

In addition to retirement benefits, Social Security offers workers both life and disability insurance. Journalist Marta Russell cites a 1996 government study that found that only one in four private sector employees were covered by long-term disability insurance. Since then, work-related coverage has shrunk. She explains:

[T]here is no private insurance plan that can compete with a social insurance program such as [Social Security disability insurance] in covering disabled workers. For a twenty-seven-year-old worker with a spouse and two children, for instance, Social Security provides the equivalent of a $353,000 disability insurance policy. The vast majority of workers would be unable to obtain similar coverage through private markets.[11]

More generally, Social Security insures against risks that the private sector will not insure against. Peter Diamond and Peter Orszag observe: "In particular, one cannot insure in the private insurance market against the risk that one's career will not turn out as expected; such insurance is typically available only from government programs like Social Security."[12]

Summary
Social Security is a well-run and highly respected government program. Its structure, which has stood the test of time, is financially responsible and consistent with basic American values. Criticisms of the system are exaggerated and sometimes untrue. Social Security is not facing bankruptcy. In fact, there is enough money in the trust funds to pay promised benefits for many years to come. Although Social Security is taking in less money than it needs to pay future retirees, the shortfall is not a "crisis" and can be made up without changing the system's basic structure. Furthermore, Social Security not only helps retirees avoid poverty but also offers the kind of protection to workers and their families that cannot be found in the private sector.

Social Security Does More Harm Than Good

The "grandfather clause" was a notorious means of preventing African Americans from voting in the post–Civil War South. State laws established strict qualifications for voting, such as paying a poll tax and passing a literacy test, but exempted those residents whose grandfather had voted. All of those exempted were white. Michael Kinsley, a columnist at Slate.com, finds a similarity between Social Security and the grandfather clause: both favor an older and established class of citizens over the rest of the population. Kinsley explains why such laws get passed:

> The appeal of grandfather-clause politics to politicians is obvious. The people enjoying some benefit now are going to be more attached to it than those who may get it in the future. People are more attached to advantages they enjoy now than to advantages they themselves

will be due in the future. Grandfather-clause politics is a way to buy off the noisiest elements of opposition among voters, or even within individual voters.[1]

Powerful interest groups support the status quo.

AARP, formerly known as the American Association of Retired Persons, is one of the most powerful voices in the debate over Social Security. The advocacy group, which claims more than 40 million members over the age of 50, strongly opposed President George W. Bush's plan to reform Social Security. Critics cite AARP as a classic example of a special interest group. After the Bush proposal died, Howard Gleckman and Mike McNamee of *BusinessWeek* observed: "This isn't the first issue in which questions have arisen over whether AARP's commercial interests may conflict with those of its members. In 2003 it backed Bush's controversial plan to remake Medicare. Liberals claimed AARP's support was driven more by its interest in selling Medicare insurance than by the interests of its members."[2] Economist Robert Samuelson argues that an "entitlements crisis" has arisen because we spend too much on programs for older Americans. He assigns most of the blame to AARP.

AARP is not the only interest group that opposes Social Security reform. Liberal organizations have also fought against reform. Many of those organizations have ties to the Democratic Party, which is committed to preserving the status quo. The platform adopted at the party's 2008 national convention said: "We reject the notion . . . that Social Security is a disgrace; we believe that it is indispensable. We will fulfill our obligation to strengthen Social Security to make sure it provides guaranteed benefits Americans can count on, now and in future generations. We will not privatize it."[3]

The antireform stance of most Democrats and many Republicans stems from the fact that older Americans are the most likely to vote, belong to advocacy groups, and express their views to lawmakers. In 2003, groups representing these individuals lobbied Congress to pass the Medicare prescription drug benefit. That benefit was the largest expansion of a federal entitlement program in a generation.

Peter J. Ferrara argues that the very design of Social Security creates a vicious circle that locks future generations into the system:

> When this generation retires and the next genera-tion starts to work, they face the same dilemma. They would have been better off if the program had never been started, but now that it has they must meet their liabilities to the current retired generation. If they had to pay these liabilities as well as provide for their own retirement themselves they would be even worse off, so they vote to continue the program and tax future generations to support their retirement. Generation after generation, the program continues to operate in this way.[4]

Social Security is unfair to younger workers.

In 1940, Ida Mae Fuller, a housewife from Vermont, received the first-ever Social Security check. Even though Ms. Fuller paid only $22 in taxes to the system, she collected more than $20,000 in benefits before she died at the age of 100. For years, the govern-ment held her up as a symbol of Social Security's success. Critics, however, see Fuller as an example of how unfair the system is to younger Americans. Peter G. Peterson, a leading advocate of reform, points out that between 1979 and 2004, median income in households of persons aged 65 or older rose by one-third, while the median income of those younger than 45 remained flat: "What phase of life today experiences the lowest poverty rate? Answer: the elderly, of whom only 10.4 percent are officially poor. In the mid-seventies, the elder poverty rate plunged below the rate for children; and since the mid-nineties, it has been trending beneath the rate for working-age adults as well."[5]

In 1980, Peter J. Ferrara warned that Social Security's finances were deteriorating, and explained its impact on workers: "In its new, mature stage, social security is impoverishing American workers, particularly young workers now entering the program. It is preventing these young workers from accumulating large

QUOTABLE

President George W. Bush

In his 2005 State of the Union address, President George W. Bush warned that Social Security needed major structural changes:

> Thirteen years from now, in 2018, Social Security will be paying out more than it takes in. And every year afterward will bring a new shortfall, bigger than the year before. . . . By the year 2042, the entire system would be exhausted and bankrupt. If steps are not taken to avert that outcome, the only solutions would be drastically higher taxes, massive new borrowing, or sudden and severe cuts in Social Security benefits or other government programs. . . .

> We must make Social Security permanently sound, not leave that task for another day. . . . As we fix Social Security, we also have the responsibility to make the system a better deal for younger workers. And the best way to reach that goal is through voluntary personal retirement accounts. Here is how the idea works. Right now, a set portion of the money you earn is taken out of your paycheck to pay for the Social Security benefits of today's retirees. If you are a younger worker, I believe you should be able to set aside part of that money in your own retirement account, so you can build a nest egg for your own future.

> Here is why personal accounts are a better deal. Your money will grow, over time, at a greater rate than anything the current system can deliver— and your account will provide money for retirement over and above the check you will receive from Social Security. In addition, you'll be able to pass along the money that accumulates in your personal account, if you wish, to your children or grandchildren. And best of all, the money in the account is yours, and the government can never take it away.

Source: George W. Bush, State of the Union Address, February 3, 2005. http://www.cnn.com/2005/ALLPOLITICS/02/02/sotu.transcript.

retirement funds. . . . It is preventing them from enjoying much higher benefits and higher standards of living in retirement."[6] Since then, Social Security has become an even worse bargain. Peter G. Peterson explains: "A single male with average earnings who retired in 1965 received lifetime Social Security benefits that were worth an 8.5 percent annual real return on his lifetime payroll taxes. A single male who retired in 2000 is projected to receive a 1.6 percent return. A single male who will retire in 2030 is projected to receive a return of just 1.0 percent."[7] Peterson and other reformers contend that these workers would earn a much higher return if they were allowed to invest their payroll taxes in stocks and bonds.

Critics use language such as "intergenerational theft" to describe Social Security. Robert Samuelson objects strongly to a system that allows retirees with very high incomes to receive both a pension and subsidized medical care—and, at the same time, forces younger, lower-earning Americans to pay for their elders' benefits. Critics also argue that the contract between generations was entered into long before today's workers had a chance to vote on it. That, in Peter J. Ferrara's opinion, amounts to taxation without representation:

> It is simply incredible that government officials are today trying to induce young people to base their future financial security on promises that seem at this point to be unreliable. Social security is usually perceived as a humanitarian institution, but there is nothing humanitarian about inducing an entire generation of Americans to rely on benefit promises that may never be paid.[8]

Social Security is unfair to the working poor.

Critics argue that Social Security and other federal programs help middle-class Americans with political influence, not the poor who most need help from the government. Political economist Mancur Olson observes:

Most of the redistribution of government is not from upper-income or middle-income people to low-income people. Most of the redistribution of income in fact is from middle-income people to other middle-income people, or from the whole of society to particular groups of rich people, or from one group to another where the groups are distinguished not by one being poor and the other being rich, but only by the fact that some groups are organized and some are not.[9]

Critics also allege that Social Security's finances are unfair to poorer Americans. The system relies heavily on a payroll tax that takes 6.2 percent of every worker's wages, starting with the first dollar earned. This tax falls most heavily on lower-earning workers because wages account for most of what they earn. Most higher-earning workers have interest and dividend income, which is not subject to the payroll tax. They are also more likely to own assets (such as homes, stocks, and bonds) that appreciate in value over the long term. There is no Social Security tax on the increase in their value. Social Security also exempts wages above $106,800 a year. In 2007, more than one-sixth of all wages—all of it paid to the highest-earning workers—went untaxed. Furthermore, benefits are not "means tested." The wealthiest retiree can collect as much as $27,876 a year in benefits without proving that he or she needs the money. Thus working- and middle-class Americans end up subsidizing wealthy retirees.

Social Security also contributes to "asset poverty"—low-earning workers' inability to save enough money to acquire assets and thus build wealth. Asset poverty deprives these workers of the chance to buy a home, start a business, or send their children to college. Critics call the payroll tax a major contributor to asset poverty because it consumes money that workers could have set aside for themselves. Social Security benefits also cannot be passed on to one's children because the Social Security account does not belong to the worker, and monthly benefit checks stop when the worker dies. Jagadeesh Gokhale, a senior economic adviser with the Federal Reserve Bank of Cleveland, explains how Social Security helps lock the working poor into a cycle of poverty:

> Social Security increases inequality of bequeathable wealth within each generation. This occurs because Social Security reduces the ability and the incentive of low earners to accumulate personal savings for retirement. In addition, greater inequality of retiree wealth due to meager wealth accumulation by low earners prevents their children from receiving sizable inheritances. This means that such children have a greater likelihood of themselves retiring with low bequeathable wealth.[10]

Social Security is unfair to women.

Critics across the political spectrum agree that Social Security is unfair to women. Much of this unfairness results from assumptions, made in the 1930s when Social Security was created, that the man would be the family wage earner and the woman would be a wife and mother. In 1971, a Social Security advisory council rejected the idea of survivor benefits for widowed men: "A man generally continues to work to support himself and his children after the death or disability of his wife. The Council therefore does not recommend that benefits be provided for a young father who has children in his care."[11] It took a ruling by the U.S. Supreme Court to force the government to abandon that policy.

Social Security works against nontraditional women in several ways. It pays benefits to surviving spouses and children of workers who die before retiring. Women who stay single, or who marry but have no children, have to pay for those benefits, which others will receive and they will not. Social Security is unfair to working women in two ways. First, they earn less than men. In 2008, the U.S. Department of Labor reported that women who worked full time earned only about 80 percent as much as men who worked full time. Second, women are less likely than men to work a full career because they are more likely to take time off to raise children or care for family members. Lower pay and lost years of work combine to reduce these women's benefits in retirement. Some married women's career earnings are so low that they qualify for a higher Social Security benefit based on their husband's earnings than on their own. In effect, those women receive nothing in return for the payroll taxes they paid.

FROM THE BENCH

Weinberger v. Wiesenfeld, 420 U.S. 636 (1975)

During the 1970s, the U.S. Supreme Court handed down several decisions striking down laws that treated men and women differently. *Weinberger v. Wiesenfeld* was one such decision. It grew out of a challenge to a provision of the Social Security Act that granted survivors' benefits to widowed women but not widowed men. The disparity stemmed from Congress's assumption in 1939, when it added survivor benefits to the Social Security Act, that a man would be the primary source of financial support for his family. As late as 1971, a federal advisory council on Social Security rejected the idea of survivor benefits for men because the father's "customary and predominant role" was to work, not to stay home and care for his children.

In 1972, Stephen Wiesenfeld's wife, Paula, died during childbirth. While the couple was married, Paula worked as a teacher and was the family's primary wage earner. After Paula died, Stephen applied for Social Security benefits for himself and his young son, Jason. The local Social Security office approved Jason's survivor benefits, but told Stephen that he was ineligible. Wiesenfeld sued the government on behalf of himself and other widowed men who were denied benefits. He argued that treating widowed men and women differently violated the U.S. Constitution. The government argued that since Social Security benefits were not compensation for work done, it had no obligation to give widowed men the same benefits as widowed women. It also argued that the law was designed to benefit women, especially widows, who tended to have less wealth and less ability to earn money in the workplace.

Even women who do not work fulltime are shortchanged by the system. Many of them perform unpaid labor, such as volunteer work or caring for family members, to which Social Security assigns a value of zero.

Social Security is unfair to minorities.

Because minorities are more likely to be unemployed or under-employed, they generally qualify for a smaller retirement benefit from Social Security. If they can find steady work, they are more

The U.S. Supreme Court declared the law unconstitutional. Justice William Brennan wrote the Court's opinion. He concluded that the law was unfair to women like Paula Wiesenfeld because their contributions to the Social Security system resulted in less protection for their families than men's contributions: "[I]n this case social security taxes were deducted from Paula's salary during the years in which she worked. Thus, she not only failed to receive for her family the same protection which a similarly situated male worker would have received, but she also was deprived of a portion of her own earnings in order to contribute to the fund out of which benefits would be paid to others."

Justice Brennan also pointed out that Social Security benefits were based on how long a person worked and how much he or she earned, not on need: "Since [Social Security] benefits do depend significantly upon the participation in the work force of a covered employee, and since only covered employees and not others are required to pay taxes toward the system, benefits must be distributed according to classifications which do not without sufficient justification differentiate among covered employees solely on the basis of sex."

Finally, Justice Brennan concluded that even a law with a benevolent purpose had to comply with the Constitution. In this case, the law under challenge did not comply because the entire structure of survivor benefits was based on the assumption that widowed women would stay home to care for their children but widowed men would go back to work. Because that assumption discriminated among children solely on the basis of the surviving parent's sex, he found it irrational.

likely to spend their careers working in low-paying jobs. In addition, under Social Security's benefit formula, a person who works as little as 10 years in a high-paying job can receive as much in retirement as a person who works a full 35-year career in a low-paying job. Furthermore, future payroll tax increases or benefit cuts, which will inevitably happen if Social Security is not reformed, will have the greatest impact on women and members of minority groups because they generally earn less than white males.

Critics argue that Social Security is especially unfair to African-American men, who have a lower life expectancy than their white counterparts. The President's Commission to Strengthen Social Security explains:

> One egregious failing of the present system is its effect on minorities with shorter life spans than the white majority. For black men age 20, only some 65 percent can be expected to survive to age 65. Thus, one of every three black youths will pay for retirement benefits they will never collect.... And because Social Security provides no property rights to its contributors—the Supreme Court has twice so ruled—a worker could easily work forty years then die and own not a penny of the contributions he has made for retirement benefits he will never collect. There are, to be sure, survivors and dependents benefits, but many workers die before eligibility for these is established. Disability insurance was added during the Eisenhower Administration so that workers are covered during their working years. But far too many never receive any retirement benefits and leave no estate.[12]

Summary

Well-organized interest groups have so far prevented Social Security reform. These groups have prevailed upon elected officials to maintain the status quo, which is unfair to millions of Americans. Social Security benefits older Americans at the expense of younger workers, who will receive less in benefits than what they contributed. The working poor lose a greater portion of their wages to payroll taxes than high earners, and this prevents them from saving money and building wealth for themselves and their families. Social Security assumes that women will be wives and mothers, which discriminates against women in nontraditional roles. Social Security is also unfair to members of minority groups, who often have below-average career earnings and shorter life expectancies and thus collect less in benefits.

Social Security Helps Millions of Americans

Supporters point out that Social Security is not just a system of old-age pensions but also an interlocking series of social-insurance programs. They warn that changes to the pension system proposed by reformers could undermine the rest of the system. Authors Peter Diamond and Peter Orszag explain why supporters consider Social Security a unique and irreplaceable federal program:

> To sum up, Social Security has certain core principles, including the following: to provide benefits to workers and their families in the form of a real annuity after the disability, retirement, or death of a family wage earner; to provide higher annual benefits relative to earnings for those with lower earnings; and to provide similar

replacement rates on average to cohorts that are close in age.[1]

Social Security made retirement possible.

A civilized society cares for the vulnerable members and respects the elderly. For those reasons, most countries have established programs designed to provide citizens with enough income to retire with dignity after a lifetime of work. In the United States, the Social Security Act was a major step in that direction. Nancy Altman, the head of the Center for Pension Rights, says: "Prior to the enactment of Social Security, most people saw retirement on an adequate income as an impossible dream. With the promise of Social Security, it became a realistic goal."[2]

Today, more than 60 percent of older nonworking Americans have chosen to retire. Financial security gives these retirees the freedom to choose free time over paid work. Nancy Altman explains: "People who have independent income have more freedom, not less. They can choose where they want to live rather than going, hat in hand, to family members. Social Security beneficiaries have the freedom from worry that comes with a stable source of income. Independence and financial security in the aftermath of misfortune and in old age are blessings that exist today largely because of Social Security."[3]

Social Security is considered one of the "four pillars" of retirement security; the other three are pensions and savings, working after reaching retirement age, and health insurance. Social Security is the most reliable of the four. Less than half of working Americans have a pension plan where they work; personal savings have been at an all-time low for many years; and nearly 50 million Americans lack health insurance, while millions more have inadequate coverage. Social Security has also "democratized" retirement, making it possible for working people of all classes to enjoy it. Retirement has taken its place alongside the eight-hour day, weekends, and paid holidays as something working Americans have come to expect.

Social Security has reduced poverty.

During the Great Depression, the national unemployment rate peaked at nearly 25 percent, more than twice what it was during 2010. Older Americans were especially prone to losing their jobs. In his majority opinion in *Helvering v. Davis,* a 1937 case, Justice Benjamin Cardozo wrote of the problem: "In times of retrenchment, the older [workers] are commonly the first to go, and even if retained, their wages are likely to be lowered. The plight of men and women at so low an age as 40 is hard, almost hopeless, when they are driven to seek for reemployment."[4]

In the Great Depression, many older Americans not only lost their jobs but also saw their life's savings disappear after the stock market crashed and banks failed. Frequently their grown children could not support them because they, too, were out of work. The elderly poor were forced to rely on the charity of others—strangers, in many cases—in order to survive. Today, "going to the poorhouse" is a figure of speech, but in the days before Social Security, that institution actually existed. Living conditions in such places resembled those of prisons more than homes, and those sent there lost their dignity and privacy. One of Justice Cardozo's reasons for upholding the Social Security Act was that it provided older Americans greater peace of mind by lessening the chances that they would end up in the poorhouse.

According to the Social Security Administration (SSA), only 9.7 percent of older Americans are below the poverty line today. That is the lowest rate of poverty of any age group. Much of the credit goes to Social Security benefits, which according to the SSA are paid to 87 percent of Americans age 65 or older. For many older Americans, Social Security is their last line of economic defense. In 2007, the SSA reported that Social Security provided at least half the income of 53 percent of older couples; 73 percent of the income of unmarried older individuals; 90 percent or more of the income of 21 percent of couples; and 44 percent of the income of individuals. Some observers believe that half of older Americans would be living in poverty were it not for Social Security.

Social Security provides benefits to non-retired Americans as well. By one recent estimate, Social Security provided the equivalent of disability insurance worth $230,000 and life insurance worth $354,000. The SSA, which calls the system "America's Family Protection Plan," explains:

> In fact, about 1-in-3 Social Security beneficiaries is not a retiree. Almost nine million workers and family members get disability benefits, and about 6-1/2 million people get monthly survivors benefits. These benefits can make a significant difference. For example, a 35-year-old worker with expected lifetime average earnings of $40,000 a year and who has a spouse and children could get about $1,890 a month from Social Security if he or she became disabled. If that same worker were to die, his or her family could receive about $2,480 a month from Social Security in survivors benefits.[5]

Social Security helps women, children, and minorities.

Social Security's progressive benefit formula helps women offset their typically lower lifetime earnings. Because of its "gender neutrality," women's benefits are not reduced to reflect their longer life expectancy. Benefits are indexed to inflation, which is important to women who, on average, live three years longer than men. Social Security also protects workers' children and spouses. According to Nancy Altman, this aspect of the system has greatly helped women:

These provisions have prevented millions of children who have lost parents from being engulfed in poverty. They permit [women] who stay home to care for children, and so reduce their own earnings, to have reasonable standards of living when the workers on whom they depend grow old, become disabled, or die. And the protections have been amended to

FROM THE BENCH

Charles C. Steward Machine Company v. Davis, 301 U.S. 548 (1937) and Helvering v. Davis, 301 U.S. 619 (1937)

When the Social Security Act was signed into law in 1935, there were serious doubts as to whether the U.S. Supreme Court would find it constitutional. Conservative justices, who held a narrow majority on the Court, believed that the Constitution gave the federal government a limited role in regulating the nation's economy.

The Supreme Court decided two cases involving challenges to the act's constitutionality on May 24, 1937. By then, one member of the Court's conservative bloc had begun voting to uphold laws aimed at combating the Great Depression. His vote created a majority that found the act constitutional.

The first case, Charles C. Steward Machine Company v. Davis, challenged the act's unemployment insurance program. The company argued that the new law violated constitutional limitations on Congress's taxing power and also violated the Tenth Amendment because the federal government exercised power that properly belonged to the states. By a 5 to 4 vote, however, the Court found the law constitutional.

Justice Benjamin Cardozo wrote the majority opinion. He first concluded that the employer tax did not violate constitutional restrictions on the taxing power because the tax was uniform and not discriminatory. Cardozo next concluded that funding a national system of unemployment compensation was a proper exercise of Congress's constitutional power to "provide for the general welfare." He wrote: "It is too late today for the argument to be heard with tolerance that in a crisis so extreme the use of the moneys of the nation to relieve the unemployed and their dependents is a use for any purpose narrower than the promotion of provide the same financial protection to dependent spouses who become divorced after many years of marriage.[6]

Critics often argue that Social Security shortchanges members of minority groups, especially African-American men who have lower career earnings and shorter life expectancies and

---

the general welfare. . . . The nation responded to the call of the distressed." Finally, Cardozo concluded that the unemployment-insurance system did not intrude on the states' constitutional powers. Even though the law imposed conditions that a state had to meet, those conditions were reasonably related to protecting the unemployed.

The second case, *Helvering v. Davis*, challenged Social Security's old-age pension system. As in *Steward*, Justice Cardozo concluded that the pension system was constitutional. He said that the general welfare was not a static concept—what was "critical" or "urgent" changes with the times. Cardozo noted that the Depression had hit older Americans especially hard. Not only was the number of older Americans growing but also an increasing number of them could no longer provide for themselves. One major reason was unemployment: In hard times, older workers are often the first to be laid off; and even if they keep their jobs, their wages are likely to be cut. He observed: "With the loss of savings inevitable in periods of idleness, the fate of workers over 65, when thrown out of work, is little less than desperate." He cited the findings from a recent study of the Social Security Board that found "one-fifth of the aged in the United States were receiving old-age assistance, emergency relief, institutional care, employment under the works program, or some other form of aid from public or private funds; two-fifths to one-half were dependent on friends and relatives, one-eighth had some income from earnings, and possibly one-sixth had some savings or property. Approximately three out of four persons 65 or over were probably dependent wholly or partially on others for support." Turning to the pension system itself, Cardozo said, "Rescue becomes necessary irrespective of the cause. The hope behind this statute is to save men and women from the rigors of the poor house, as well as from the haunting fear that such a lot awaits them when journey's end is near."

therefore get less in retirement benefits. Paul Krugman, a professor at Princeton University, responds:

> First ... [b]lacks' low life expectancy is largely due to high death rates in childhood and young adulthood. African-American men who make it to age 65 can expect to live, and collect benefits, for an additional 14.6 years—not that far short of the 16.6-year figure for white men.
>
> Second, the formula determining Social Security benefits is progressive: it provides more benefits, as a percentage of earnings, to low-income workers than to high-income workers. Since African-Americans are paid much less, on average, than whites, this works to their advantage.
>
> Finally, Social Security isn't just a retirement program; it's also a disability insurance program. And blacks are much more likely than whites to receive disability benefits.[7]

As traditional pensions disappear, Social Security has become even more important.

Until 1980, almost all company pension plans were of the defined-benefit variety. Defined-benefit plans provide a retired worker with a fixed monthly pension, the amount of which is based on earnings. The typical plan pays a retired worker a percentage of his or her average earnings for the last few years of work. To pay these benefits, the employer contributes cash and other assets, such as corporate stock, into a pension fund. Workers value defined-benefit plans because they provide a predictable amount of income in retirement. When added to Social Security, the company pension helps make a comfortable retirement possible.

Defined-benefit pensions, however, are disappearing as a number of large corporations have gone bankrupt. Even though a federal agency, the Pension Benefit Guarantee Corporation, provides workers and retirees at these corporations with some protection, it lacks the funds to restore lost pensions in their entirety. Many other corporations face large unfunded liabilities. According to the Mercer consulting firm, the nation's 1,500 largest companies' plans were underfunded by 25 percent, or $409 billion, at the end of 2008. To avoid underfunding, some companies have "frozen" their plans, limiting the amount that current workers will receive when they retire. Throughout the country, companies are phasing out defined-benefit plans in favor of defined-contribution plans, which do not guarantee workers a specific level of income in retirement. Employers favor defined-contribution plans because they contribute a fixed amount (if any) and need not worry about underfunding.

Today, workers run the risk that their employer will go out of business. Defined-contribution plans create the additional risk that a falling stock market will wipe out their pension and force them to work past retirement age. Teresa Ghilarducci observes:

> If more people had defined benefit plans, some of these feelings of insecurity would be tempered and the economy would be more stable. Instead of older people having to work more when the economy slows, they could gradually phase out of working, as older people tended to do in past recessions. Social Security, of course, does not depend on stock and bond prices to pay out a steady and secure income.[8]

Critics who accuse the government of being biased toward defined-contribution plans point out that the federal tax code encourages employers to switch to these accounts. In 2004, the federal government gave employers $115 billion a year in tax breaks for having contributed to their employees' 401(k)

(continues on page 74)

Defined-benefit and Defined-contribution Pensions

One major issue in the debate over Social Security involves the merits of "defined-benefit" versus "defined-contribution" pension plans. Social Security follows the traditional defined-benefit model, while personal accounts follow the defined-contribution model.

At one time, almost all pension plans were defined-benefit plans, in which an individual who meets certain criteria becomes entitled to a fixed amount of money at retirement. That amount is usually paid monthly. Most government employees and many workers at large corporations—especially where workers belong to a labor union—still have defined-benefit plans.

In 1980, the federal government allowed employers to establish 401(k) plans for their workers. The name comes from the section of the federal tax code that governs the accounts. These are called defined-contribution plans because the amount invested in the worker's account is fixed, but the amount the worker receives in retirement depends on how much was invested in the account and how well the investments performed.

Those who prefer traditional pensions contend that defined-contribution plans leave employees vulnerable to the ups and downs of financial markets. Supporters of defined-contribution plans counter that traditional plans are financially unsustainable and were designed for a time when workers spent their entire career at the same company.

Employers are not required to establish a pension plan, although there are tax benefits for employers that do.

Characteristics of a Defined-benefit Plan:

- The employer contributes to the pension fund. The contributions are part of the worker's "package" of benefits.
- The employer is responsible for funding the plan and making the investments needed to provide income for retired workers.
- The pension fund is managed by the employer or by a financial institution selected by the employer.
- The amount of the worker's pension is based on age, years of service, and total earnings.
- The worker does not own the money the employer has set aside for retirement.

- Workers usually must work a minimum number of years to qualify for a pension. This requirement exposes workers to "employment risk," the possibility they will not work long enough to collect a pension.
- Pensions are guaranteed by a federal agency, the Pension Benefit Guaranty Corporation.

Characteristics of a Defined-contribution Plan:

- Workers have the option of contributing to a plan, but do not have to do so.
- The worker contributes a percentage of his or her wages to the account. Many companies, but not all, match at least part of the worker's contribution.
- The worker pays no income tax on money invested in the account. Instead, taxes come due when the worker draws the money, presumably in retirement when he or she is in a lower tax bracket.
- The worker has a range of choices where to invest the money in the account. Most accounts are managed by private financial institutions.
- The worker is responsible for investment decisions and bears the risk of market fluctuations.
- There is no employment risk because the account is "portable": the worker still owns the money even after leaving his or her current employer.
- A worker may withdraw money from the account before retirement under certain circumstances, such as buying a first home. However, early withdrawal usually results in a tax penalty.

In Both Plans, Workers Are Exposed to the Following Risks:

- Employer risk—the possibility that the employer will go bankrupt. A worker enrolled in a defined-benefit plan can avoid this risk by not investing in shares of his or her employer's stock.
- Poverty risk—the possibility that benefits will not be enough to keep the worker above the poverty line.
- Political risk—the possibility that changes in the tax code or other federal laws will reduce the value of the pension.

(continued from page 71)
accounts. Most of those contributions went into high-income workers' accounts. Ghilarducci explains:

> The IRS allows 401(k) participants to invest pretax income, deferring taxes until retirement. The tax subsidy is equal to the investment earnings on the deferred taxes, which depends on the marginal tax rate paid by a household. A wealthy family in the 35% tax bracket gets a tax break three-and-a-half times more valuable than a lower-income family in the 10% tax bracket, even if each family contributes the same dollar amount to a 401(k) plan. This is extremely biased, since it is much harder for a low-income household to save than it is for a wealthy household.[9]

Not only do 401(k) plans widen the gap between high-earning and low-earning workers, but they also increase the federal deficit because they encourage higher earners to contribute as much as possible in order to reduce their tax bill.

The baby boomers need Social Security.

Many Americans took what they thought were prudent steps: they bought a home and invested in the stock market. During the first decade of the twenty-first century, however, both home prices and the stock market suffered steep declines. By some estimates, $15 trillion in wealth disappeared. The baby boom generation, which ranged in age from the mid-forties to the mid-sixties, suffered some of the worst losses. At the same time the baby boomers suffered a massive loss of wealth, many of them also lost their jobs because of the recession. Some never went back to work, while others took new jobs that paid much less.

The baby boom generation faces the prospect of working longer and harder than their parents. According to an AARP researcher, Americans older than 55 have stepped up their participation in the labor force, often in jobs with poor working conditions. A Government Accountability Office economist found that workers who leave retirement and reenter the labor force take lower-paying jobs than their career jobs, suggesting that these older workers have been "pushed" into the workforce by economic circumstances, not "pulled" from retirement by high wages. Some economists believe that these low-paid older workers also drag down wages for workers of all ages.

Many baby boomers are not financially ready to retire. The Securities Industry Association recently estimated that about 45 percent of this generation will be unable to replace 60 percent or more of their preretirement income in retirement. Economist Dean Baker explains:

> The sudden collapse in the wealth of baby boomer households shows the need for establishing more secure savings vehicles for the country's workers. Traditional defined-benefit pension plans did shield workers from the sort of market fluctuations that decimated the value of 401(k) and other defined contribution plans in the last two years. However, defined benefit plans are rapidly dwindling in the private sector. Many of the plans that are still surviving are also struggling as a result of the recent downturn in the market. Employers will find it very costly to restore these plans to proper funding levels.[10]

The baby boom generation will be even more dependent on Social Security than their parents were. For that reason, Dean Baker believes it is a matter of economic justice to preserve the system:

> The idea of taking away Social Security benefits from baby boomers was always outrageous. After all, this is a generation that has paid into Social Security at the

current 12.4 percent tax rate for almost their entire working life and will be forced to wait until age 66 or even 67 to get full benefits. Their average returns are projected to be lower than the generations that follow and far lower than the generations that preceded them.[11]

Summary
Social Security has greatly reduced poverty among older Americans and allowed millions of working Americans to enjoy a dignified retirement. Social Security also provides financial security to spouses and children of workers who die. It gives added protection to women and members of minority groups, who often have below-average incomes. Social Security will become even more important in the years to come. Today's near-retirees face an uncertain future because traditional pension plans are disappearing from the workplace, and the recession that began in late 2007 has forced many of these individuals to work at low-paying jobs and left them with little in retirement savings.

Personal Accounts Are Superior to Social Security

German chancellor Otto von Bismarck was a staunch conservative, but he nevertheless introduced old-age pensions in his country. Niall Ferguson, a professor at Harvard University, explains that Bismarck had an ulterior motive—namely, "to engender in the great mass of the unpropertied the conservative state of mind that springs from the feeling of entitlement to a pension." Ferguson goes on to say, "To the surprise of his liberal opponents, Bismarck openly acknowledged that this was 'a state-socialist idea! The generality must undertake to assist the unpropertied.' But his motives were far from altruistic. 'Whoever embraces this idea,' he observed, 'will come to power.'"[1]

Social Security is obsolete.

Paul Kasriel, the director of economic research at Northern Trust Company, considers Social Security obsolete:

> The current social security model . . . was adopted dur-
> ing the Great Depression as a welfare program for the
> aged. During the Great Depression, those senior citizens
> who were able to work could find little employment.
> And many of those seniors who had saved for their
> retirements or had pensions found their nest eggs
> greatly reduced because of the depressed economy and
> the stock market crash of 1929. So, a welfare program
> for the aged, established during the Great Depression,
> persists today.[2]

Social Security has serious flaws. To begin with, it is financed
by a payroll tax that not only falls most heavily on low-earning
workers but stifles economic growth as well. In 2008, this tax
accounted for 83 percent of Social Security's revenue. The Social
Security Act also requires that assets in the Social Security trust
funds be invested in a special series of Treasury bonds. That
requirement, which dates back to 1935, limits the trust funds
to a 2 to 4 percent return on its investment, compared to an
average 7 to 10 percent return on corporate stocks and bonds.
Another more serious flaw of Social Security is that it is a "pay-
as-you-go" system: payments to current beneficiaries are made
from current revenue. That was not the original design of the
Social Security Act. Its drafters intended to create a large reserve
out of which benefits would be paid. In 1939, however, Congress
moved up the date for paying benefits and increased benefit
amounts. Consequently, the large reserve never materialized.
Social Security also follows a defined-benefit model, meaning
that retirees are promised a fixed monthly amount. In fact,
unlike company pensions, Social Security benefits are adjusted
to keep up with inflation. Because the number of current and
future retirees is growing while the number of workers is shrinking, Social Security faces unfunded liabilities estimated to be in
the trillions of dollars. That shortfall is much larger than the
unfunded liabilities of all corporate pension funds combined.

Peter J. Ferrara contends that a true trust fund has enough assets to pay beneficiaries strictly out of investment earnings. Depending on the rate of return, those assets must be 10 to 15 times as large as the payments the fund makes each year. At the end of 2008, however, the Social Security trust fund had $2.24 trillion on hand and paid $625 billion in benefits, for a ratio of about 3.6 to 1. That ratio will drop sharply as the aging baby boomers retire. The trust funds contain so little money that Ferrara called them "merely cash flow accounts to which the money sits only long enough for benefit checks to be written."[3]

Social Security is risky.

The government calls payroll taxes "contributions" and refers to workers' "accounts," creating an impression that Americans are guaranteed Social Security benefits when they retire. That is not the case. The President's Commission to Strengthen Social Security warned:

> While the defined benefit formula does not subject individuals to financial market uncertainty, the formula itself can be changed and has been changed in the U.S. numerous times in the past. This political risk to benefits is all the more real because the Social Security system faces perpetual financing deficits starting in the middle of the next decade, such that currently scheduled benefits cannot be paid.[4]

Even though Social Security is called an "entitlement program," there is no constitutional right to receive benefits. In the 1960 case of *Flemming v. Nestor*, the U.S. Supreme Court ruled that treating benefits as a property right would deprive the Social Security system of the flexibility it needs to adjust to changing conditions. The Court noted that Congress reserved to itself the power to change or repeal any portion of the Social Security Act. Thus whether workers will receive Social Security

Retirees' raises

*Annual cost-of-living increases
to monthly Social Security
checks since the system was
linked to the Consumer Price
Index in 1975:*

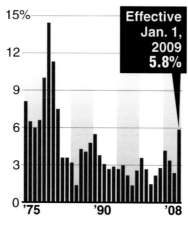

Effective
Jan. 1,
2009
5.8%

© 2008 MCT
Source: U.S. Social Security Administration

This chart shows the annual cost-of-living increases to monthly Social Security checks since 1975 when the system was first linked to the Consumer Price Index. In 2008, the Social Security Administrated adjusted cost-of-living upward by 5.8 percent for 2009.

depends on the willingness of future taxpayers to keep support-ing the system. For that reason, Peter J. Ferrara likens Social Security to a Ponzi scheme, an investment scam that pays early investors with money put in by later investors rather than profits earned by the investment. A Ponzi scheme collapses when it runs out of new investors.

Reformers also contend that the Social Security trust fund holds no real assets. George Schultz, a former secretary of the Treasury, explains:

> The Social Security trust fund contains the surpluses, invested in government bonds, that have been generated by the system since its inception. One purpose of this trust fund is to help pay for future benefits. However, it will not be of much help for the eventual solvency of Social Security because the money that Social Security has transferred to the Treasury has not been saved but rather used to pay the day-to-day expenses of running the government. The bond purchases have built up to a bundle of federal government IOUs.[5]

Once Social Security starts paying more in benefits than it collects in revenue, reformers warn, Social Security's trustees will present the bonds in the trust funds to the U.S. Treasury, which will then have to either raise taxes or borrow money to redeem them.

Personal accounts encourage self-reliance.

Critics argue that social insurance makes citizens dependent on the government or, worse yet, the political party that promises the most generous benefits. Peter G. Peterson, a former secretary of commerce, argues that Social Security was driven by politics from the very beginning:

> [E]ven during his lifetime, President Roosevelt knew just what he was doing. When asked about the inability of his trust funds to effect genuine savings, he once answered, "Those taxes were never part of economics. They are politics all the way through. We put those payroll taxes there so as to give the contributors a legal, moral, and political right to collect their pensions. . . .

With those taxes there, no damn politician can ever scrap my social security program."[6]

Once Social Security was created, it became a permanent fact of political life. Powerful interest groups such as AARP support its continued existence, and members of Congress fear the political consequences of changing it.

FROM THE BENCH

Flemming v. Nestor, 363 U.S. 603 (1960)

During the 1950s, Congress ordered the deportation of noncitizens who had belonged to the Communist Party and terminated their Social Security benefits. Ephram Nestor, who came to this country from Bulgaria in 1913, was deported and stripped of his benefits because he had been a Communist during the 1930s. At the time, there were no laws against joining the party. Nestor sued the government, claiming that the termination of his benefits was unconstitutional. He argued that he had reached retirement age, and therefore his Social Security benefits had become a property right the government could not summarily take away. Nestor also argued that the government violated the Constitution by punishing him after the fact for having been a Communist.

Nestor's lawsuit reached the U.S. Supreme Court. In *Flemming v. Nestor*, the Court upheld the termination of his benefits. The vote was five to four. Justice John Harlan, who wrote the majority opinion, concluded that Social Security "was designed to function into the indefinite future," and went on to say: "To engraft upon the Social Security system a concept of 'accrued property rights' would deprive it of the flexibility and boldness in adjustment to ever-changing conditions which it demands." For that reason, he noted, Congress had reserved the right to "alter, amend, or repeal any provision" of the Social Security Act.

Justice Harlan next concluded that the government had not deprived Nestor of due process of law. Denying benefits violated due process only when it was based on "a patently arbitrary classification, utterly lacking in rational justification." In this case, Congress reasonably could terminate Nestor's benefits because he was now living overseas. Harlan said: "One benefit which may be thought to accrue to the economy from the Social Security system is the increased over-all national purchasing power resulting from taxation of productive elements of the

Social Security was never intended to be retirees' only source of income. In fact, President Roosevelt himself expected workers to supplement Social Security checks with their own retirement savings. Today, however, millions of older Americans are effectively dependents of the government through Social Security. The Cato Institute argues: "In effect, Social Security turns older Americans into supplicants, dependent on the political process for

economy to provide payments to the retired and disabled, who might otherwise be destitute or nearly so, and who would generally spend a comparatively large percentage of their benefit payments."

Finally, Harlan concluded that the government had not punished Nestor, let alone violated the constitutional restrictions on punishment. Deportation was not punishment, but rather an exercise of Congress's power to determine which non-citizens could enter and remain in the United States. Nor was the termination of benefits a form of punishment—despite its financial impact on Nestor—because it simply flowed from Congress's decision to change eligibility standards.

The four dissenting justices argued that the government violated the Constitution when it terminated Nestor's benefits. In their view, the laws that triggered the loss of benefits were *ex post facto* laws, which punished past conduct that was legal at the time it occurred. Even though Nestor had not suffered criminal penalties, he nevertheless was punished because he lost what "may well be this exile's daily bread" simply because he had once a member of the Communist Party. The dissenters also argued that the government had deprived Nestor of property without due process of law and called the termination of Nestor's benefits an unconstitutional *bill of attainder*, an act of the legislative branch singling out a specific and identifiable group of people—in this case, former Communists—for punishment. Justice William Brennan, one of the dissenters, observed: "Today's decision sanctions the use of the spending power not to further the legitimate objectives of the Social Security program but to inflict hurt upon those who by their conduct have incurred the displeasure of Congress. The Framers ordained that even the worst of men should not be punished for their past acts or for any conduct without adherence to the procedural safeguards written into the Constitution."

their retirement benefits. If they work hard, play by the rules, and pay Social Security taxes their entire lives, they earn the privilege of going hat in hand to the government and hoping that politicians decide to give them some money for retirement."[7]

Personal retirement accounts, on the other hand, are consistent with the American values of individual liberty and self-reliance. They are an integral part of an "ownership society" in which Americans are rewarded for hard work and thrift. Personal accounts are also safer than Social Security. They are less subject to political risk because it is more difficult for the government to "raid" them to pay for federal programs. Because workers own the accounts, they are less prone to "employer risk," that of the employer freezing or ending a company pension plan, or "employment risk," that of losing one's job. Both are important considerations in today's turbulent economy.

Personal accounts will benefit the economy.

Rahm Emanuel, a former member of Congress who became President Barack Obama's chief of staff in 2009, says: "Every American who works ought to have the chance to save. But today, too many don't. . . . In addition, Americans don't start saving early enough. The typical American starts working at age 22, but on average, most do not begin to participate in an employer savings plan until age 41—losing 19 years of savings."[8] The 2006 Retirement Confidence Survey found that only 60 percent of American workers said they were saving for retirement. Inadequate saving for retirement is part of a larger problem. In 1994, a bipartisan commission on entitlement programs noted that countries with high savings and investment rates grow faster and have higher standards of living than countries with low savings and investment rates. It warned that private savings had fallen so low that the nation's productivity and growth were in danger. Since then, the problem has grown worse. In recent years, the nation's savings rate fell to near zero, although savings have been on the rise since the economic recession began in late 2007.

Personal accounts would encourage workers to save more for retirement. That is especially true of low-earning workers, who would likely get money from the government to invest in their accounts. In 2001, Professor Michael Sherraden told the President's Commission to Strengthen Social Security:

> For the vast majority of households, the pathway out of poverty is not through income and consumption but through saving and accumulation. . . . When people begin to accumulate assets, their thinking and behavior changes as well. Accumulating assets leads to important psychological and social effects that are not achieved in the same degree by receiving and spending an equivalent amount of regular income.[9]

The commission also cited studies that linked asset ownership to a heightened sense of financial well-being and greater willingness to plan for the future.

An original objective of the Social Security Act was to encourage older workers to retire, freeing jobs for younger Americans seeking work. Social Security still encourages early retirement despite the fact that people live longer and spend more years in retirement. Personal accounts would encourage people to work longer and retire later, giving a boost to the economy. The President's Commission to Strengthen Social Security explains: "Near retirement, workers may perceive that accumulations in their accounts will grow, and the annuities they can purchase will increase, if they work and contribute longer. This may encourage them to stay in the labor force—an incentive that becomes particularly important as Baby Boomers retire."[10]

Personal accounts are a proven success.

During the 1970s, Chile's government asked American free-market economists to help it overhaul a failing social-insurance system. The economists proposed replacing the country's pension system with a system of personal accounts. Professor Niall Ferguson contends that the experiment was a success:

> [T]he pension reform not only created a new class of property owners, each with his own retirement nest egg. It also gave the Chilean economy a massive shot in the arm, since the effect was significantly to increase the savings rate (to 30 per cent of GDP by 1989, the highest in Latin America). . . . The annual rate of return on the Personal Retirement Accounts has been over 10 per

IRAs and 401(k) Plans

Personal accounts, which are a key element of most Social Security reform plans, will likely resemble Individual Retirement Accounts (IRAs) or 401(k) plans. In 2008, according to the Investment Company Institute, Americans had $3.6 trillion invested in IRAs and another $3.5 trillion in 401(k)s and similar plans.

Congress created traditional IRAs in 1974. To be eligible to contribute to an IRA, a person must be less than 70 and 1/2 years old; must have earned income; may not be enrolled in an employer-sponsored retirement plan; and must have an adjusted gross income below $44,000 ($64,000 for a married couple filing a joint income tax return). The maximum allowable contribution is $3,000 per year, although people older than 50 may contribute $3,500. If a person owns more than one IRA, the contribution limit applies to the sum of contributions to all accounts. Although IRA contributions are tax deductible, when the account owner withdraws money, both the original contribution and the money earned on it are taxable.

A person who withdraws money from an IRA before age 59 and 1/2 must pay a 10-percent penalty on the amount withdrawn in addition to the income tax itself. The penalty is not imposed if the account owner suffered a disability, became unemployed and used the money to buy health insurance, or used the money to pay for college tuition or a first home.

cent, reflecting the soaring performance of the Chilean stock market, which has risen by a factor of 18 since 1987. . . . The poverty rate has declined dramatically to just 15 per cent, compared with 40 per cent in the rest of Latin America.[11]

Ferguson also notes that Chile's economic reform fueled economic growth as well. During the 15 years before reform, the country's annual growth rate was only 0.17 percent, but during the 15 years that following reform, it was 3.28 percent. Other countries have followed Chile's example. The President's

In 1997, Congress created Roth IRAs to allow workers to pay taxes during their working years, rather than in retirement when they can least afford the tax bill. To be eligible to contribute to a Roth IRA, a person must have an adjusted gross income below $110,000 ($160,000 for a married couple filing a joint income tax return). There is no age restriction on participating. As with traditional IRAs, the maximum allowable contribution is $3,000 per year and people older than 50 may contribute $3,500. If a person owns more than one Roth IRA, the contribution limit applies to the sum of contributions to all accounts. The tax consequences of Roth IRAs are the opposite of traditional IRAs. Contributions to these accounts are taxed, but distributions are tax free after the owner has held the account for five years and either reaches age 59 and 1/2, dies, becomes disabled, or uses the money to buy a first home.

In 1978, 401(k) accounts were created. They became popular after the Internal Revenue Service issued a ruling in 1980 that clarified their tax status. To be eligible to contribute, a person must work in the private sector. The maximum allowable contribution is $12,000 ($14,000 for those age 50 or older). As in the case of traditional IRAs, contributions are tax deductible but distributions are taxed. The account owner may take a distribution at age 59-1/2 (earlier if the owner leaves his or her job, the employer terminates the plan, or in case of financial hardship). If a person has an IRA as well as a 401(k) account, the 401(k) limits the deductibility of the person's IRA contributions.

Commission to Strengthen Social Security found that more than 20 countries—including Mexico, Poland, and the United Kingdom—had personal accounts, and that numerous others—including Russia and China—were in the process of creating them.

Personal accounts have succeeded in this country as well. Until 1983, local governments could opt out of Social Security. Galveston County, Texas, did so in favor of a private alternative. Ray Holbrook, who at the time headed the county's government, said in 2005 that the private plan averaged an annual rate of return of 6.5 percent. He also said that the lowest-paid county workers could look forward to at least 50 percent more in retirement than under Social Security, and that higher-paid workers would do better yet: "We sought a secure, risk-free alternative to the Social Security system, and it has worked very well for nearly a quarter-century. Our retirees have prospered, and our working people have had the security of generous disability and accidental death benefits."[12]

In 1986, Congress created the Thrift Savings Program, a system of personal accounts offered to federal employees, who are not covered by Social Security. Under the plan, a federal employee could choose from among three investments: short-term Treasury bills, a corporate bond index fund, or a stock index fund. (An index fund invests in a large variety of stocks and bonds. Because their holdings are so diversified, these funds are considered a relatively safe investment.) During the 1990s, the average return was 6.7 percent for the Treasury bill fund, 7.9 percent for the bond index fund, and 17.4 percent for stock index fund. The President's Commission to Strengthen Social Security estimated that an average earner who worked from age 21 to age 65, regularly invested in the plan, and spread the investments among the three funds would end up with a balance of more than $500,000 at retirement.

Summary

Social Security's structure has not changed since 1935, when a major objective was to reduce unemployment by encouraging older workers to retire. Even though the government assures workers that they will receive benefits, there is a risk that those benefits will be cut because sufficient funds will not be available. Social Security is subject to political manipulation and makes people dependent on the government. On the other hand, personal accounts reward thrift and self-reliance, are safer than Social Security, and are a better investment. They will also benefit the economy by encouraging people to save more, invest wisely, and work longer.

Personal Accounts Are Dangerous

Teresa Ghilarducci warns that reformers want to replace Social Security with a system of "do-it-yourself retirement." For many, that will mean no retirement at all. Ghilarducci says:

> The diminishment of Social Security is part of the attack on retirement entitlement. With personal savings accounts, there will be no secure form of pension. Insecure pensions mean more work. The increase in work effort will likely come from individuals who most depend on Social Security as the way they will need to fund retirement. The meaning of retirement will be debased if it is a forced working retirement.[1]

Ghilarducci goes on to warn that personal accounts would transform Social Security from an earnings-based insurance system, in which benefits to retirees are based on their working lifetime earnings, into an income replacement program for the elderly poor—in other words, a form of welfare. That is not what President Roosevelt had in mind when he signed the Social Security Act.

Chile's experiment was a failure.

Reformers call Chile's system of personal accounts a success and urge American lawmakers to follow its example. Circumstances, however, were different in Chile. To begin with, its pension system was a shambles. That system had a deficit equal to 25 percent of the country's GDP, and 93 percent of retirees received only the minimum pension benefit. In addition, personal accounts were part of a wide-ranging reform of that country's financial markets, which were primitive in comparison to ours. It should also be noted that the Chilean government that privatized pensions was a military dictatorship that committed serious human rights violations, including torturing and killing its opponents.

Some believe that Chile's experiment with personal accounts was a failure. The Century Foundation, a progressive organization, says:

> A quarter of a century since privatization took effect, Chilean's retirement security is on shaky ground. Recent reports by the World Bank and the Federal Reserve have highlighted some of the many problems with Chile's system. A combination of high management fees, low participation rates, unexpectedly heavy dependence on an inadequate safety net, and prohibitively high costs to government have led the system along a path of failure and left many Chilean workers with no reliable retirement plan. Is this really the model the United States hopes to replicate?[2]

Chile's personal accounts were run by private financial institutions that charged huge administrative costs, in some cases as much as one-third of workers' contributions. The brokerage firm CB Capitales found that after commission charges, the average account earned just 5.1 percent a year between 1982 and 1999—not 11 percent as claimed by the government. It also said that the average worker would have done better by investing his or her pension fund contributions in a passbook savings account. Furthermore, many personal accounts performed so badly that they could not even provide a minimum pension. As a result, the government had to make up the difference, which made the program much more costly than expected. Even with government subsidies, 40 percent of retirement-age Chileans had to keep working to make ends meet.

Personal accounts create risk and uncertainty.

The success of both Galveston's pension-fund experiment and the federal Thrift Savings Plan resulted from an unusually strong stock market. Between March 1980 and October 2007, the Standard and Poor's (S&P) 500 stock index rose more than 1,600 percent. Stocks rarely perform that well for so long. In fact, stocks can—and often do—lose value. Since 1990, the S&P 500 has suffered an annual decline of 10 percent or more in one year out of five. Sometimes stocks fall much more sharply than that. Between October 2007 and March 2009, the S&P 500 fell by 57 percent. The steep decline was devastating to near-retirees who had invested in stocks for their retirement and now had just a few preretirement years in which to make up their losses. Some near-retirees fared even worse. They lost their jobs in the recession and had to withdraw money from already-depleted retirement accounts to make up for lost income.

Because Social Security was designed to insulate older Americans from risk, revenue in the trust funds is invested in U.S. government bonds, which are unaffected by the rise or fall of stock prices. Substituting personal accounts for traditional Social Security would reintroduce risk into older Americans'

retirement plans. Gary Burtless of the Brookings Institute stud-
ied the incomes of hypothetical workers who invested 2 percent
of their earnings in stock index funds over a 40-year career.
Burtless found that the "replacement rate"—the percentage of
preretirement income the worker will receive in retirement—
varied widely depending on when a worker retired. It ranged
from 17 percent for those who retired in 1974, when stocks were
in an extended slump, to 39 percent for those who retired in
March 2000, at the height of the Internet stock bubble. By comparison, Social Security is projected to replace 35 to 40 percent
of preretirement income.

The risk of personal accounts is made even worse by many
account owners' lack of investment skill. People are especially
prone to overestimate how well their investments will perform.
Dean Baker observes: "Even after the stock market crash of
2000–2002, most families continued to under-estimate the risk
associated with holding stock. Clearly they were encouraged
in this attitude by many professional investment analysts who
promoted stocks as financial assets that were associated with
relatively little risk if held for a long enough period of time."[3]

Many Americans are ignorant about finances in general.
In 2004, researchers at the University of Michigan asked baby
boomers a simple math problem requiring knowledge of com-
pound interest. Only 18 percent answered it correctly. About half
did not know that investing in a variety of stocks was safer than
investing in just one stock. And women, who on the average live
longer than men, were more likely to underestimate their life
expectancy and thus risk outliving their retirement income.

For these reasons, Teresa Ghilarducci concludes that personal accounts are a bad risk: "The personal savings account
plan does not provide independence from government, does not
assure earning a higher rate of return, and does not escape from
a flagging Social Security system. In short, it does not make a
worker's retirement pension income any more secure."[4]

Reformers have a hidden agenda.
Many supporters of reform are likely to benefit from the creation of these accounts. They would be a bonanza for the financial-services industry, which is already one the nation's most powerful

Social Security Facts and Figures

Who is receiving Social Security benefits?
According to the Social Security Administration (SSA), as of December 2008:

- About 48.3 million were receiving old age or disability benefits only, 4.9 percent were receiving Supplementary Security Income (SSI) benefits, and 2.6 million were receiving benefits from both programs.

- About four-fifths of those receiving old age, survivor, or disability benefits were age 62 or older, 24 percent were age 75 to 84, and 10 percent were older than age 85. About 15 percent were between the ages of 18 and 61 and were receiving benefits as disabled workers, survivors, or dependents. Another 6 percent were younger than age 18.

- Of all adults receiving monthly Social Security benefits, 56 percent were women and 44 percent were men. Seventy-eight percent of the men and 59 percent of the women were receiving old age benefits. About one-fifth of the women were receiving survivor benefits.

In 2008, 5.1 million Americans were added to the benefit rolls. (Beneficiaries who either died or lost their eligibility offset that figure.) Forty-four percent of the new beneficiaries were retired workers, 17 percent were disabled workers, and the remaining 39 percent were survivors or the spouses and children of retired or disabled workers.

As of 2007, 88 percent of married Americans and 86 percent of unmarried Americans age 65 or older were receiving Social Security benefits. Social Security was the "major source" (more than half) of the total income of 53 percent of married couples older than 65, and for 73 percent of unmarried individuals older than 65. It provided 90 percent or more of income for 21 percent of married couples older than 65 and for 44 percent of unmarried individuals older than 65.

special interests. Brokerages, insurers, and other companies make large profits administering workers' 401(k) plans and stand to make even larger profits managing personal accounts. In fact, under such reform, many of the same companies whose reckless

How has the Social Security program grown over the years?

In 1937, the first year benefits were paid, 53,236 beneficiaries received $1.28 million. In 2000, 45.4 million beneficiaries received $408 billion.

How much do beneficiaries receive?

In 2009, the maximum Social Security benefit was $2,323 per month for a worker who retired at full retirement age. As of December 2008, the average monthly Social Security benefit was $1,054, and average monthly SSI payment was $478. The average male beneficiary received $1,274 per month, and the average female beneficiary $962.

How much do workers and their employers have to pay in Social Security taxes?

Currently, the payroll tax on both the worker and his or her employer is 6.2 percent of wages: 5.3 percent for the Old Age and Survivors Insurance (OASI) program, and 0.9 percent for the Disability Insurance (DI) program. In 2010, the Social Security Wage Base, the maximum amount of wages subject to payroll taxes, was $106,800. Thus the maximum amount of payroll taxes that can be deducted from a worker's wages is $6,622 per year. The average worker pays $3,216 per year.

How much money is in the Social Security Trust Fund?

In 2009, the SSA estimated that the OASI and DI Trust Funds had a combined balance of $2.56 trillion. That same year, the trust funds took in a combined total of $819.4 billion. Of that amount, 83 percent came from payroll taxes, 2 percent from income taxes on Social Security benefits, and 14 percent from interest earned on the government bonds held by the trust funds. The trust funds paid out $682.5 billion, leaving a surplus of $136.9 billion for the year. Administrative costs for the trust funds were 0.9 percent of contributions.

Sources: Social Security Administration. *Update 2010.* Washington, D.C., 2010; Social Security Administration. *Fast Facts & Figures About Social Security, 2009.* Washington, D.C., 2009.

decisions caused a worldwide financial crisis in 2008 would manage workers' accounts. Teresa Ghilarducci notes: "Employer-based defined benefit pensions were once regarded as an important aspect of the productive life in the nation, at least for two-thirds of full-time workers. However, 401(k) plans have become profitable for consulting firms, actuaries, pension lawyers, money managers, all pension vendors, and employers."[5]

Economist Dean Baker points out that Peter Peterson, a leading supporter of personal accounts, made billions of dollars managing a private mutual fund. Baker accuses Peterson of favoring his friends on Wall Street over workers and retirees:

> The public would be right to be outraged that a Wall Street billionaire is trying to take away the core social insurance programs that they will be dependent on in their old age. It was the Wall Street crew that wrecked the economy, costing millions of people their jobs and tens of millions their life savings. Now Peterson wants to use much of his Wall Street winnings to take away the only source of support that tens of millions of retirees have left.[6]

During the past 30 years, such defined-contribution plans have replaced defined-benefit plans at many corporations. Some view this trend as part of a "race to the bottom," in which companies maximize profits by reducing workers' wages and cutting back on benefits. Corporations support defined-benefit pension plans because those plans limit their obligation to future retirees and, at the same time, reduce their tax bill. They likewise favor Social Security reform because it would reduce their payroll tax bill. Corporate executives have added reason to support personal accounts. Because they earn considerably higher salaries, they will be able to contribute more to those accounts and will receive still more money in retirement because less of their wages will go to Social Security, whose progressive benefit structure favors lower-earning workers.

The transition to personal accounts would be difficult.

A shift to personal accounts would entail huge transition costs. Simply put, the government would have to pay for two systems at once: personal accounts for working Americans' retirement and traditional Social Security for retirees and near-retirees. The financial impact would be huge. A week after George W. Bush's 2005 State of the Union address, which urged the creation of personal accounts, Federal Reserve chairman Alan Greenspan admitted to Congress that diverting payroll taxes to those accounts would more than double the Social Security System's 75-year financial shortfall. Teresa Ghilarducci observes: "Most scholars agree that the high transition costs will probably doom any transformation of a mature pay-as-you-go system—a system we know by the name of Social Security—to a system entailing personal savings accounts."[7]

Personal accounts would also create a logistical nightmare. Tens of millions of accounts would have to be created almost overnight. Managing them would require a huge and expensive bureaucracy run by the Social Security Administration, private companies, or both. Dallas Salisbury, the head of the Employee Benefits Research Institute, estimated that it would conservatively require a decade and a staff of 100,000 workers to administer a universal system of private accounts. Most reform plans allow workers to divert some, but not all, of their payroll taxes to a personal account. Thus the Social Security Administration's workload would actually increase if it had to oversee workers' personal accounts.

Personal accounts raise other concerns as well. Administrative costs would reduce the value of personal accounts, as they have in Chile and Great Britain. Letting private companies manage personal accounts would also be an invitation to fraud and abuse. During the 1990s, British regulators uncovered a "mis-selling" scandal that involved hundreds of thousands of retirement accounts. They found that sales agents knew too little about their customers to give them sound advice and used high-pressure sales tactics to get them to switch to inappropriate account plans. In addition, if workers could move back and forth between traditional Social Security and personal accounts, some might try to outguess the stock market and make bad investment decisions. Finally, there is no assurance that workers will use their personal accounts to fund their retirement. The tax code allows owners of 401(k) accounts to make "hardship

What Is "Indexing"?

In most years since Social Security was created, the economy has experienced inflation—rising prices of goods and services. Inflation has serious consequences for those who receive fixed incomes because each monthly check has less buying power than the one before it.

In 1950, Congress increased Social Security benefits to compensate for inflation that had occurred since the system was created. This 75-percent increase was the first-ever "cost of living allowance" (COLA). During the 1950s and 1960s, lawmakers approved a series of *ad hoc* COLAs so that benefits could keep pace with inflation. In 1972, Congress amended the Social Security Act to make COLA automatic, beginning in 1975. Every January, benefits are adjusted upward by a percentage equal to the Consumer Price Index (CPI), the government's measure of the price of basic household goods and services. For that reason, the increases are referred to as "indexing." Indexing does not apply to benefits alone. The Social Security Wage Base, the maximum amount of wages subject to payroll taxes, is also adjusted every year for inflation. In 2010, that figure stood at $106,800.

Another form of indexing is used to determine a worker's Average Indexed Monthly Earnings (AIME). Wages earned during all but the last two years before withdrawals" to pay for a new home or college tuition. Congress will likely face pressure to allow similar hardship withdrawals from personal retirement accounts, which would defeat their purpose.

Reform could end Social Security altogether.

Many believe that the push for Social Security reform is part of conservatives' "starve the beast" strategy. They want to cut taxes, which would inflate the federal budget deficit, then point to those deficits as a justification for reducing the size of the government. Grover Norquist, a leading conservative figure, once said, "My goal is to cut government in half in twenty-five years . . . to get

the worker reached age 62 are indexed to reflect the increase in *wages* nationwide. Since wages have risen faster than prices, wage indexing results in higher initial benefits than price indexing.

Most observers agree that indexing benefits protects beneficiaries from losing purchasing power. Some, however, contend that indexing creates a vicious cycle: higher benefits lead to increased federal spending, which, in turn, contributes to inflation.

Indexing *initial* benefits to reflect wage increases, rather than price increases, is more controversial. A federal commission warned Congress that this practice would make Social Security financially unsustainable. Instead, it recommended indexing benefits to prices. Congress ignored the warnings and, in 1977, adopted the current policy of indexing initial benefits to wage growth. As a result, initial benefit levels are 19 percent higher than they would have been otherwise—between 1977 and 2008, the national average wage index calculated by the Social Security Administration rose 423 percent, while the CPI rose 355 percent. Critics insist that wage-indexing initial benefits will become an even bigger financial burden once tens of millions of baby boomers reach retirement age. Supporters, however, insist that wage indexing is fair because wages reflect higher productivity and believe that those workers who improved productivity should be rewarded.

it down to the size where we can drown it in the bathtub."[8] Federal entitlement programs are at the top of conservatives' list of targets because they are not just large but also symbols of "big government." One prominent pro-reform voice is the Cato Institute, which is philosophically opposed to the concept of Social Security and whose experts have long argued for personal accounts. Several members of the President's Commission to Strengthen Social Security had ties to the Cato Institute.

Personal accounts, like 401(k)s, will further widen the gap between well-off and poor workers. As Teresa Ghilarducci pointed out, 401(k) plans favor high-earning workers. Once high earners realize how lucrative personal accounts are, they will demand the right to opt out of Social Security altogether. Advocates also warn that reformers' "carve-out" approach, which would divert part of workers' payroll taxes into personal accounts, would make Social Security less of a retirement system and more of a social-insurance program. That, in turn, might lead middle-class voters to see Social Security as "just another welfare program" and stop supporting it. Their opposition to Social Security could also have racial overtones. As Peter Diamond and Peter Orszag observe, "The bottom line is that Social Security provides crucial social insurance protections to minorities, and substantially scaling back the Social Security program would impose disproportionate harm on minorities."[9]

Some believe that the weakening of Social Security through reform would have consequences for American workers that go far beyond retirement. Journalist Marta Russell warns: "If workers were provided with a federal social safety net that adequately protected them through unemployment, sickness, impairment, and old age, then business would have less control over the work force because labor would gain a stronger position from which to negotiate their conditions of employment, such as fair wages, reasonable accommodations, and flexible work hours."[10]

Summary

Chile's experiment with personal accounts was a failure that left workers and retirees even worse off. Social Security reform would have the same result here. Personal accounts are dangerous and would expose workers to the ups and downs of the stock market and add to the risks that accompany aging. Those accounts would benefit powerful financial institutions, along with well-paid workers who already benefit from employer-provided retirement plans. Personal accounts entail huge transition costs that would increase the budget deficit, and the accounts themselves would be expensive to administer. Personal accounts would further widen the gap between lower- and higher-earning workers—and might even endanger Social Security itself by converting it into a welfare program with little political support.

Social Security's Future

From modest beginnings, Social Security has become the largest nondefense federal government program. In 1940, when the first checks were issued, slightly more than 220,000 Americans received benefits. That total has grown to more than 50 million, or one in six Americans. Nevertheless, Social Security's basic structure remains as it was when the program began. Reformers argue that if Franklin Roosevelt were still alive, he would be astonished that Social Security's structure has not changed after 75 years. Defenders of the current system counter that it has stood the test of time. The President's Commission to Strengthen Social Security observed:

> From the first, Social Security was a work in progress. It remains so now. In 1939, just four years after enactment, the Administration and Congress added major

provisions. FDR called for more. As he signed the 1939 Amendments he stated: "we must expect a great program of social legislation, as such as is represented in the Social Security Act, to be improved and strengthened in the light of additional experience and understanding." He urged an "active study" of future possibilities.[1]

An Overview of the Debate

In her book *When I'm Sixty-Four,* Teresa Ghilarducci maintains that seven issues that were debated in the 1930s are still being debated today:

1. How long should older Americans work?
2. What should the federal government do when employer pension funds fail?
3. Will longer life spans make the Social Security system insolvent?
4. Does Social Security diminish Americans' initiative to plan for their own retirement?
5. Can Social Security and employer-based retirement systems lessen inequality in both income and wealth?
6. If a crisis occurs, will major reform be necessary?
7. Is a pre-funded program or a pay-as-you-go program more affordable?

The Status of the Reform Movement

President Bush's proposal to divert part of Social Security payroll taxes to personal accounts died in Congress. The 2006 and 2008 elections did not help the reformers' cause. They gave the Democratic Party—whose elected officials generally oppose major Social Security reform—control of the presidency and both houses of Congress. In recent years, Social Security has taken a backseat to more pressing problems such as preventing the banking system from collapsing, getting Americans back to work, and reforming the nation's health care system.

In 2009, the Cato Institute said: "Although President Bush failed in his effort to reform Social Security, the problems facing our national retirement system have not gone away. In fact, since the demise of the Bush proposal, Social Security's long-term unfunded liabilities have increased by more than $550 billion, and now total $15.3 trillion."[2] In January 2010, Paul Ryan, a member of Congress from Wisconsin, wrote a column

The Greenspan Commission's Recommendations

In 1981, President Ronald Reagan issued an executive order to create the National Commission on Social Security Reform. This was a 15-member bipartisan commission headed by economist Alan Greenspan, who later became chairman of the Federal Reserve. The president directed the commission to analyze the financial condition of the Social Security trust funds, identify problems that may threaten those funds' long-term solvency, and propose solutions to those problems to the president and Congress.

In 1983, the commission issued its report. It concluded: "Congress should not alter the fundamental structure of the Social Security program or undermine its fundamental principles." The commission considered, but rejected, proposals to make Social Security voluntary, change it into a program under which benefits were based exclusively on contributions paid, or change it to a program under which benefits would be based on financial need.

The commission did offer 22 recommendations for reforming the existing system, including:

- Requiring civilian employees of the federal government and employees of nonprofit organizations to participate in Social Security.

- Making half of a person's Social Security benefits subject to federal income tax if his or her adjusted gross income, not including Social Security, is $20,000 or more.

- Increasing the contribution of self-employed people by approximately one-third.

in the *Wall Street Journal* in which he offered a "Republican road map" to economic recovery.[3] Ryan's proposals included personal retirement accounts and a gradual, modest increase in the retirement age.

Even President Barack Obama, President Bush's Democratic successor, realizes that the federal government cannot postpone Social Security's reform forever. Shortly after taking office in

- Basing annual cost-of-living adjustments to benefits on the lower of price increases and wage increases when the Social Security trust fund balance is low, but allowing "catch-up" adjustments when the fund balance is high.

- Levying Social Security and Medicare payroll taxes on wages paid into an employee's 401(k).

- Creating a "fail-safe" mechanism to ensure that benefits are paid on time despite "unexpectedly adverse conditions which occur with little advance notice." Possibilities include short-term borrowing from the U.S. Treasury, allowing the trust funds to issue their own bonds and sell them to the public; or temporarily raising the payroll tax, the maximum taxable earnings base, or both.

- Removing the Social Security and Medicare trust funds from the "unified budget" of the federal government. This practice, which began in 1969, understated the size of the federal deficit because the trust funds have enjoyed annual cash surpluses.

- Make the Social Security Administration (SSA) an independent agency. In 1983, the SSA was part of the Department of Health and Human Services (DHHS), even though it had a larger budget and more employees than the rest of DHHS combined.

Sources: Executive Order 12335, *Federal Register*, Volume 46, p. 61633 (December 18, 1981); National Commission on Social Security Reform. *Report of the National Commission on Social Security Reform.* Washington, D.C.: Government Printing Office, 1983. http://www.socialsecurity.gov/history/reports/gspan.html.

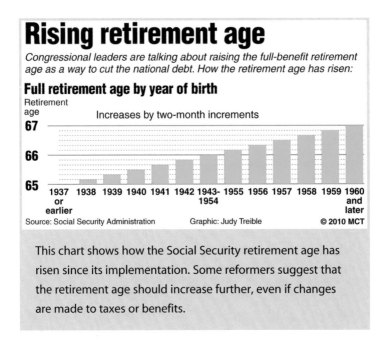

Rising retirement age

Congressional leaders are talking about raising the full-benefit retirement age as a way to cut the national debt. How the retirement age has risen:

Full retirement age by year of birth

Retirement age

Increases by two-month increments

| Retirement age | 1937 or earlier | 1938 | 1939 | 1940 | 1941 | 1942 | 1943-1954 | 1955 | 1956 | 1957 | 1958 | 1959 | 1960 and later |

Source: Social Security Administration   Graphic: Judy Treible   © 2010 MCT

This chart shows how the Social Security retirement age has risen since its implementation. Some reformers suggest that the retirement age should increase further, even if changes are made to taxes or benefits.

January 2009, he said: "What we have done is kicked this can down the road. We are now at the end of the road and are not in a position to kick it any further. . . . We have to signal seriousness in this by making sure some of the hard decisions are made under my watch, not someone else's."[4]

Entitlements, Deficits, and Debt

In his 1999 State of the Union address, President Bill Clinton asked Congress to use part of the federal budget surplus to shore up Social Security. Lawmakers rejected the idea, and it is unlikely that another surplus will soon be available to shore up the system. After 1999, the nation's financial picture changed dramatically for the worse, and Congress added to the problem by cutting taxes and adding programs such as the Medicare prescription drug benefit. Instead of a surplus, the federal government expects to run a deficit of $1.3 trillion in fiscal 2011. Years of deficit spending have resulted in a national debt of more than $13.8 trillion, a figure that is likely to rise further. In February 2010, the Congressional Budget Office projected deficits totaling $9.7 trillion in the coming decade.

Reformers blame Social Security and other entitlement programs for the nation's deteriorating finances. Peter G. Peterson remarks:

> We all recall the old philosophy riddle: "What happens when an irresistible force meets an immovable object?" At least one answer to that conundrum lurks somewhere in America's not-so-distant future. The irresistible force is benefit growth in entitlement programs. This growth is automatic. It is linked to the upward march of wages and medical prices, and to the aging of the population. It is scheduled to happen even if Congress never passes another law.... The immovable object is taxes.[5]

Some economists, like Lawrence Kotlikoff, believe that the nation's finances are even worse than the government says they are. Kotlikoff cites a 2005 study by economists Jagadeesh Gokhale and Kent Smetters that concluded that the United States government had a "fiscal gap"—the difference, in today's dollars, between all future revenues and all future expenditures—of $65.9 trillion. Most of that gap is the result of entitlement programs. Unless those programs are reined in, he warns, an economic catastrophe will occur. Kotlikoff explains that because lawmakers are reluctant to raise taxes, cut benefits, or even limit the growth in benefits, the government is left with only one alternative—namely, "printing money," which is what occurs when the government buys back Treasury bills and bonds. He goes on to explain what could happen next:

> [O]nce the financial markets begin to understand the depth and extent of the country's financial insolvency,

they will start worrying about inflation and about being paid back in watered-down dollars. This concern will lead them to start dumping their holdings of U.S. Treasuries. In so doing, they'll drive up interest rates, which will lead the Fed to print money to buy up those bonds. The consequence will be more money creation—exactly what the bond traders will have come to fear. This could lead to spiraling expectations of higher inflation, with the process eventuating in hyperinflation.[6]

Hyperinflation means a rapid increase in prices—sometimes by hundreds of percent a year—because the government has issued so much paper money that it has lost its value. America has never experienced hyperinflation, but many other countries have. One of them is Argentina, which has been on the verge of bankruptcy for almost a century. In fact, during the 1990s, Argentina defaulted on its bonds, causing billions of dollars in losses to investors all over the world. Kotlikoff explains: "Argentina remains in this sorry state for a good reason. Its creditors—primarily each successive generation of elderly citizens—force the government to retain precisely those policies that perpetuate the country's destitution."[7]

Payroll Taxes and Social Security's Long-term Health

Teresa Ghilarducci observes:

Every time Congress passes a [Social Security] tax increase, the increase is supposed to make the system solvent for seventy-five years. The Social Security system has been insolvent for a total of twenty-two years since 1935. Only after it becomes insolvent does Congress hike payroll taxes. The history of Social Security funding makes clear that deficits are routine and expected. Nevertheless, Congress must "manually" raise FICA taxes because the taxes are not indexed to benefits, nor to costs, nor to any measure of solvency.[8]

The combined payroll tax for employers and workers stands at 12.4 percent. According to the SSA, the system has a shortfall of 2 percent of payroll, meaning that another 2-percent increase is needed to pay promised benefits over the next 75 years. A generation ago, Peter J. Ferrara warned that there was a limit to voters' acceptance of payroll tax hikes: "It is hard to imagine taxpayers accepting social security taxes that will consume one-fourth to one-third of their paychecks. This would be two to two and one-half times current tax rates. Taxes at these rates are a far cry from the maximum $60 per year that prevailed over the first fifteen years of the program."[9]

Reform Based on Personal Accounts

Under most reform plans, a portion of the money taken out of workers' paychecks in the form of Social Security contributions would be diverted into workers' personal accounts. This is known as the "carve-out" approach. Within the reform community, there are differences of opinion as to how much should be diverted into personal accounts, who should manage these accounts, what kinds of investments would be allowable, and whether a worker should be allowed to withdraw everything from the account at retirement or receive a monthly benefit for life. Reformers also have differing opinions as to whether the government should help account owners who had made bad investments.

In 2001, the President's Commission to Strengthen Social Security offered three reform models, each of which contained some form of personal account. The most far-reaching option was "Model 2," which would give workers the option of investing 4 percent (out of 6.2 percent) of their payroll tax contributions into a personal account. Income from that account would replace most of the traditional Social Security benefits the worker would lose under reform. At retirement, workers would receive some income from personal accounts—"Social Security Part B"—and some from the traditional system—"Social Security Part A." The commission maintained that the Parts A and B, added together, would provide more income in retirement than traditional Social Security alone.

Teresa Ghilarducci disagrees with the commission. She warns that personal accounts will leave many Americans worse off:

> Workers are taking on more risks for no gain. The shift from defined benefit to defined contribution plans and

Recommendations of President Bush's Reform Commission

Shortly after taking office in 2001, President George W. Bush created the President's Commission to Strengthen Social Security. He directed the members of that panel to recommend reform plans that met the following criteria:

- Social Security benefits for retirees or near-retirees will not be changed.
- The entire Social Security surplus must be dedicated to Social Security only.
- Social Security payroll taxes must not be increased.
- The government may not invest Social Security funds in the stock market.
- Disability and survivor benefits must be contained.
- The plans must include personal accounts.

The commission offered three reform models in its December 2001 report:

- **Model 1**, which would establish voluntary "carve-out" personal accounts. A worker could invest 2 percent of his or her wages in a personal account. In exchange, the worker's traditional Social Security benefits would be reduced in proportion to the amount contributed the decline in income replacement rates from Social Security have required workers to shoulder more risk. Workers already bear the risk of being too old to work, being laid off, or being disabled. Inflation, longevity, financial and employment risks, once pooled by larger entities, are now borne by the individual.[10]

If reform becomes a reality, many older Americans might end up living in the kind of poverty that afflicted that age group during the Great Depression.

to the personal account. Aside from the carve-out accounts, the basic structure of Social Security would not change.

- **Model 2**, which would also establish voluntary carve-out personal accounts. A worker under the age of 55 could voluntarily invest 4 percent of his or her payroll taxes (out of 6.2 percent), up to $1,000 a year, in a personal account. In exchange, traditional Social Security benefits would be reduced. Social Security would also be made more progressive by increasing minimum benefits for low-earning workers who had worked at least 30 years, and by increasing minimum benefits for surviving spouses. (Note: Many observers believe that President Bush favored Social Security reform along the lines of this model.)

- **Model 3**, which would create a voluntary "add-on" personal account option. A worker under the age of 55 could voluntarily invest 1 percent of his or her wages in a personal account. That contribution would be matched by a 2.5 percent contribution from the government, up to maximum of $1,000 per year. In exchange, the worker's traditional Social Security benefits would be reduced. Social Security would also be made more progressive, as in Model 2, and the benefit structure would be changed to provide rewards for continuing to work and disincentives for taking early retirement.

Source: President's Commission to Strengthen Social Security. *Strengthening Social Security and Creating Personal Wealth for All Americans*. Washington, D.C., 2001.

Reform Without Personal Accounts

There are experts who believe that Social Security can be strengthened without resorting to personal accounts. Some of them favor an approach similar to the Greenspan Commission, which reformed Social Security without changing its basic structure. The added revenue needed to keep the system solvent would come from several sources: a modest raise in the payroll tax, lifting the ceiling on payroll taxes from its current level of $106,800 per year, and depositing estate tax revenue into the Social Security Trust funds.

Many reformers propose add-on retirement accounts, which would exist in addition to traditional Social Security. Some would require workers to invest a portion of their wages in add-on accounts, with the government matching those contributions. Others have suggested means testing, under which wealthier Americans would lose their eligibility for benefits. Some plans call for investing some of the Social Security trust fund assets in the stock market, and others call for "indexing" both the retirement age (raising it) and benefit levels (lowering them) to reflect longer life expectancies.

The President's Commission to Strengthen Social Security, however, maintained that reform plans without personal accounts will fail. It issued the following challenge to defenders of the current system:

> Those who believe that the share devoted to the elderly should continue to consume a larger and larger share of the nation's output have a responsibility to identify where the money will come from. Those who believe that growth in spending should be restrained have a responsibility to explain exactly how they would change Social Security's benefit structure to achieve this.[11]

The Libertarian Approach

In *The Inherent Contradiction*, Peter J. Ferrara offered a radical proposal: abolish Social Security altogether. Welfare-like elements of Social Security, such as benefits for spouses and dependents, would be transferred from Social Security to a different federal program or to private charity. The retirement element would be replaced with a system of personal accounts. Ferrara argued that if workers could keep what they paid in payroll taxes, they would have enough money to fund a retirement account and also buy life and disability insurance from private insurers.

The Cato Institute argues that many reform plans do not go far enough: "You don't cut out half a cancer. Many proposals for Social Security reform would allow workers to privately invest only a small portion of their payroll taxes, continuing to rely on the existing pay-as-you-go Social Security system for the majority of Social Security benefits."[12] Cato's plan would give workers a choice between traditional Social Security and a personal account. Those who stay in the present system would receive, in retirement, whatever benefits Social Security could pay them. Those who choose personal accounts would be given a "recognition bond" based on their past contributions to the Social Security system. That bond, plus whatever they accumulated in their personal account, would provide their retirement income.

Will a Crisis Bring About Reform?

In the early 1980s, a serious recession endangered Social Security's finances, forcing the president and Congress to take action. Many believe that the current recession will lead to a similar crisis that, in turn, would put reform back on the table. Economist Robert Samuelson, who favors reform, welcomes this prospect: "It's increasingly obvious that Congress and the president (regardless of which party is in power) will deal with the political stink bomb of an aging society only if forced. And the most plausible means of compulsion would be for Social Security and Medicare to go bankrupt: trust funds run dry; promised benefits exceed dedicated payroll taxes. The sooner this happens, the better."[13] There are signs that the crisis may arrive sooner than expected. In March 2010, the Congressional Budget Office projected that

Social Security would run deficits in fiscal years 2010 through 2013 and from 2016 onward. That projection is even more pessimistic than most experts had previously believed.

President Obama's Deficit Commission

In January 2010, in the midst of a debate on raising the national debt ceiling, a group of senators introduced a resolution, "The Bipartisan Task Force for Responsible Fiscal Action Act." The resolution would have created a task force whose mission would be drawing up a package of reforms aimed at reducing the federal deficit. Under their proposal, the task force's recommendations would go on a congressional "fast track," meaning that lawmakers could approve or reject the entire package, but could not make amendments to it. The intent of this all-or-nothing approach was to prevent lawmakers from saving their favorite federal programs from termination. Similar legislation was passed after the end of the Cold War to select military bases that were no longer needed and therefore should be closed.

The task force resolution failed to receive the required 60 votes in the Senate. Shortly afterward, however, President Barack Obama signed an executive order creating an advisory-only National Commission on Fiscal Responsibility and Reform.

The executive order directed the commission to "[identify] policies to improve the fiscal situation in the medium term and to achieve fiscal sustainability over the long run." It also directed the commission to "propose recommendations that meaningfully improve the long-run fiscal outlook, including changes to address the growth of entitlement spending and the gap between the projected revenues and expenditures of the Federal Government."[*]

The commission consisted of 18 members chosen by the president and by the Democratic and Republican leaders of both houses of Congress. The co-chairs, chosen by the president, were Erskine Bowles, a Democrat who served as chief of staff to President Bill Clinton, and Alan Simpson, a former Republican senator from Wyoming.

The commission's deadline for approving a final report was December 2010. In order to appear in the final report, a recommendation had to receive the approval of at least 14 members.

[*] Executive Order No. 13531, National Commission on Fiscal Responsibility and Reform, *Federal Register* vol. 75, p. 7927 (February 23, 2010).

As of this writing, there are signs that lawmakers are paying attention to entitlement costs. The U.S. Senate considered, but failed to approve, legislation that would have created a commission with power to propose limits on government spending. Shortly afterward, President Obama issued an executive order creating a similar commission. He directed it to "propose recommendations that meaningfully improve the long-run fiscal outlook, including changes to address the growth of entitlement spending and the gap between the projected revenues and expenditures of the Federal Government."[14] The commission's recommendations were due by the end of 2010. Among its recommendations were gradually raising the retirement age to 68 by 2050 and to 69 by 2075; increasing the limit on earnings subject to payroll taxes; and providing more generous benefits for those who worked at low-paying jobs through their careers, while scaling back benefits for high earners.

Because the president lacks the power to force Congress to act, however, the commission's recommendations might go unheeded, as was the case in 1994 after the entitlements commission created by President Bill Clinton submitted its report. Thus it remains to be seen what actions, if any, lawmakers take in response to the commission.

Summary

Social Security reformers warn that the country is headed for financial catastrophe unless it curbs spending on Social Security and other entitlement programs. Most reformers support a system that would divert part of workers' payroll tax contributions into personal accounts. Some would abolish Social Security entirely. Supporters of the current system oppose any diversion of payroll tax revenue. They believe that extra revenue can be found to keep the system solvent. Mounting federal deficits and the retirement of the baby boom generation will force lawmakers to address Social Security's finances, which have grown worse during the recent recession. The steps they take will have a profound impact on most American households.

APPENDIX ||||||▷

Beginning Legal Research

The goals of each book in the Point/Counterpoint series are not only to give the reader a basic introduction to a controversial issue affecting society, but also to encourage the reader to explore the issue more fully. This Appendix is meant to serve as a guide to the reader in researching the current state of the law as well as exploring some of the public policy arguments as to why existing laws should be changed or new laws are needed.

Although some sources of law can be found primarily in law libraries, legal research has become much faster and more accessible with the advent of the Internet. This Appendix discusses some of the best starting points for free access to laws and court decisions, but surfing the Web will uncover endless additional sources of information. Before you can research the law, however, you must have a basic understanding of the American legal system.

The most important source of law in the United States is the Constitution. Originally enacted in 1787, the Constitution outlines the structure of our federal government, as well as setting limits on the types of laws that the federal government and state governments can enact. Through the centuries, a number of amendments have added to or changed the Constitution, most notably the first 10 amendments, which collectively are known as the "Bill of Rights" and which guarantee important civil liberties.

Reading the plain text of the Constitution provides little information. For example, the Constitution prohibits "unreasonable searches and seizures" by the police. To understand concepts in the Constitution, it is necessary to look to the decisions of the U.S. Supreme Court, which has the ultimate authority in interpreting the meaning of the Constitution. For example, the U.S. Supreme Court's 2001 decision in *Kyllo v. United States* held that scanning the outside of a person's house using a heat sensor to determine whether the person is growing marijuana is an unreasonable search—if it is done without first getting a search warrant from a judge. Each state also has its own constitution and a supreme court that is the ultimate authority on its meaning.

Also important are the written laws, or "statutes," passed by the U.S. Congress and the individual state legislatures. As with constitutional provisions, the U.S. Supreme Court and the state supreme courts are the ultimate authorities in interpreting the meaning of federal and state laws, respectively. However, the U.S. Supreme Court might find that a state law violates the U.S. Constitution, and a state supreme court might find that a state law violates either the state or U.S. Constitution.

Not every controversy reaches either the U.S. Supreme Court or the state supreme courts, however. Therefore, the decisions of other courts are also important. Trial courts hear evidence from both sides and make a decision, while appeals courts review the decisions made by trial courts. Sometimes rulings from appeals courts are appealed further to the U.S. Supreme Court or the state supreme courts.

Lawyers and courts refer to statutes and court decisions through a formal system of citations. Use of these citations reveals which court made the decision or which legislature passed the statute, and allows one to quickly locate the statute or court case online or in a law library. For example, the Supreme Court case *Brown v. Board of Education* has the legal citation 347 U.S. 483 (1954). At a law library, this 1954 decision can be found on page 483 of volume 347 of the U.S. Reports, which are the official collection of the Supreme Court's decisions. On the following page, you will find samples of all the major kinds of legal citation.

Finding sources of legal information on the Internet is relatively simple thanks to "portal" sites such as findlaw.com and lexisone.com, which allow the user to access a variety of constitutions, statutes, court opinions, law review articles, news articles, and other useful sources of information. For example, findlaw.com offers access to all Supreme Court decisions since 1893. Other useful sources of information include gpo.gov, which contains a complete copy of the U.S. Code, and thomas.loc.gov, which offers access to bills pending before Congress, as well as recently passed laws. Of course, the Internet changes every second of every day, so it is best to do some independent searching.

Of course, many people still do their research at law libraries, some of which are open to the public. For example, some state governments and universities offer the public access to their law collections. Law librarians can be of great assistance, as even experienced attorneys need help with legal research from time to time.

Common Citation Forms

Source of Law	Sample Citation	Notes
U.S. Supreme Court	*Employment Division v. Smith*, 485 U.S. 660 (1988)	The U.S. Reports is the official record of Supreme Court decisions. There is also an unofficial Supreme Court ("S. Ct.") reporter.
U.S. Court of Appeals	*United States v. Lambert*, 695 F.2d 536 (11th Cir.1983)	Appellate cases appear in the Federal Reporter, designated by "F." The 11th Circuit has jurisdiction in Alabama, Florida, and Georgia.
U.S. District Court	*Carillon Importers, Ltd. v. Frank Pesce Group, Inc.*, 913 F.Supp. 1559 (S.D.Fla.1996)	Federal trial-level decisions are reported in the Federal Supplement ("F. Supp."). Some states have multiple federal districts; this case originated in the Southern District of Florida.
U.S. Code	Thomas Jefferson Commemoration Commission Act, 36 U.S.C., §149 (2002)	Sometimes the popular names of legislation—names with which the public may be familiar—are included with the U.S. Code citation.
State Supreme Court	*Sterling v. Cupp*, 290 Ore. 611, 614, 625 P.2d 123, 126 (1981)	The Oregon Supreme Court decision is reported in both the state's reporter and the Pacific regional reporter.
State Statute	Pennsylvania Abortion Control Act of 1982, 18 Pa. Cons. Stat. 3203-3220 (1990)	States use many different citation formats for their statutes.

Cases

Charles C. Steward Machine Company v. Davis, 301 U.S. 548 (1937) and Helvering v. Davis, 301 U.S. 619 (1937)

These two decisions of the U.S. Supreme Court upheld the constitutionality of the Social Security Act. The justices rejected the argument that the federal government lacked the power to establish a national system of old-age pensions and unemployment insurance.

Flemming v. Nestor, 363 U.S. 603 (1960)

The Supreme Court held that Social Security benefits were not a property right. It went on to state that Congress had broad authority to define who was eligible for benefits and how much would be paid to beneficiaries. That is still the law, even though Social Security is commonly referred to as an entitlement program.

Weinberger v. Wiesenfeld, 420 U.S. 636 (1975)

The Supreme Court held that giving benefits to widowed women, but not widowed men, was "irrational." The *Weinberger* decision reflected the Court's willingness to give closer scrutiny to laws that treat men and women differently.

Statutes

The Social Security Act of 1935

This act created what most people associate with Social Security—namely old-age benefits. It also created a system of unemployment insurance, along with what is now known as Aid for Families with Dependent Children. Even though Congress has amended the Social Security Act many times since 1935, the structure of the Social Security system is basically the same as it was when the first benefits were paid to retirees.

The Social Security Amendments of 1965

Popularly known as the Medicare Act, this legislation added two new titles to the Social Security Act: Title XVIII, which created Medicare, a program that helps pay medical bills of older Americans; and Title XIX, which created Medicaid, a program that pays for medical care for some poorer Americans.

Terms and Concepts

401(k)

"Add-on" account

Baby boom

"Carve-out" account

Consumer Price Index (CPI)

"Contract between the generations"

Cost of living allowance (COLA)

Deficits

Defined benefit

Defined contribution
Disability insurance
Entitlement program
Federal Insurance Contributions Act (FICA)
Full retirement age
General welfare
Indexing
Individual Retirement Account (IRA)
Insurance
Medicare Act
Medicare Part D
National debt
Ownership society
"Pay as you go"
Personal account
Payroll tax
Political risk
Progressivity
Savings rate
Social Security Act
Social Security wage base
Supplementary Security Income (SSI)
Survivor benefits
Tax credit
Treasury bonds
Trust fund
Unfunded liability

Introduction: The Story of Social Security

1 Squier is quoted in Nancy Altman, *The Battle for Social Security: From FDR's Vision to Bush's Gamble.* Hoboken, N.J.: John Wiley & Sons, 2005, p. 8.
2 *Ibid.*, p. 23.
3 *Ibid.*, p. 80.
4 Public Law 74-271 (49 Stat. 620), codified as 42 U.S.C. §§301 and following.
5 Franklin D. Roosevelt, Presidential Statement Signing the Social Security Act, August 14, 1935, quoted in Nancy Altman, *The Battle for Social Security: From FDR's Vision to Bush's Gamble.* Hoboken, N.J.: John Wiley & Sons, 2005, p. 83.
6 *Helvering v. Davis*, 301 U.S. 619, 644 (1937).
7 Roosevelt is quoted in Nancy Altman, *The Battle for Social Security: From FDR's Vision to Bush's Gamble.* Hoboken, N.J.: John Wiley & Sons, 2005, p. 144.
8 Social Security Amendments of 1965, Public Law 89-97 (79 Stat. 286). The act added Title XVIII of the Social Security Act, which created Medicare, as well as Title XIX, which created Medicaid, which pays for medical care for some poorer Americans.
9 Executive Order 12335, *Federal Register,* Volume 46, p. 61633 (December 18, 1981).
10 Peter J. Ferrara, *Social Security: The Inherent Contradiction.* San Francisco: Cato Institute, 1980, p. 4.
11 *Ibid.*, p. 14.
12 George W. Bush, State of the Union Address, February 3, 2005. http://www.cnn.com/2005/ALLPOLITICS/02/02/sotu.transcript.

Point: Social Security Is Unsustainable

1 Landon is quoted in Nancy Altman, *The Battle for Social Security: From FDR's Vision to Bush's Gamble.* Hoboken, N.J.: John Wiley & Sons, 2005, p. 102.
2 George W. Bush, State of the Union Address, February 3, 2005. http://www.cnn.com/2005/ALLPOLITICS/02/02/sotu.transcript.
3 Social Security Administration. *Fast Facts & Figures About Social Security, 2009.* Washington, D.C., 2009, p. 36.
4 Niall Ferguson, *The Ascent of Money: A Financial History of the World.* New York: The Penguin Press, 2008, pp. 219–220.
5 The commission is quoted in Peter G. Peterson, *Running on Empty: How the Democratic and Republican Parties Are Bankrupting Our Future and What Americans Can Do About It.* New York: Farrar, Straus and Giroux, 2004, p. 39.
6 President's Commission to Strengthen Social Security. *Strengthening Social Security and Creating Personal Wealth for All Americans.* Washington, D.C., 2001, p. 115.
7 Peter J. Ferrara, *Social Security: The Inherent Contradiction.* San Francisco: Cato Institute, 1980, p. 75.
8 President's Commission to Strengthen Social Security. *Strengthening Social Security and Creating Personal Wealth for All Americans.* Washington, D.C., 2001, p. 73.
9 George W. Bush, State of the Union Address, February 3, 2005. http://www.cnn.com/2005/ALLPOLITICS/02/02/sotu.transcript.
10 Peter A. Diamond and Peter R. Orszag, *Saving Social Security: A Balanced Approach.* Washington, D.C.: Brookings Institution Press, 2004, p. 166.
11 Menzie D. Chinn, *Getting Serious About the Twin Deficits. Special Report No. 10.* Washington, D.C.: Council on Foreign Relations, 2005, p. 3.

Counterpoint: Social Security Is a Wise Investment

1 Nancy Altman, *The Battle for Social Security: From FDR's Vision to Bush's Gamble.* Hoboken, N.J.: John Wiley & Sons, 2005, p. 3.
2 President's Commission to Strengthen Social Security. *Strengthening Social Security and Creating Personal Wealth for All Americans.* Washington, D.C., 2001, p. 68.
3 Peter A. Diamond and Peter R. Orszag, *Saving Social Security: A Balanced Approach.* Washington, D.C.: Brookings Institution Press, 2004, pp. 69–70.

4 Nancy Altman, *The Battle for Social Security: From FDR's Vision to Bush's Gamble.* Hoboken, N.J.: John Wiley & Sons, 2005, p. 315.

5 Dean Baker, "The Bankrupt Debate over Bankrupting Our Children," Truthout. com, May 11, 2009.

6 Nancy Altman, *The Battle for Social Security: From FDR's Vision to Bush's Gamble.* Hoboken, N.J.: John Wiley & Sons, 2005, p. 233.

7 Peter A. Diamond and Peter R. Orszag, *Saving Social Security: A Balanced Approach.* Washington, D.C.: Brookings Institution Press, 2004, p. 51.

8 Dean Baker, *Things That Will Happen Before Social Security Faces a Shortfall.* Washington, D.C.: Center for Economic and Policy Research, 2005, p. 2.

9 Nancy Altman, *The Battle for Social Security: From FDR's Vision to Bush's Gamble.* Hoboken, N.J.: John Wiley & Sons, 2005, p. 303.

10 *Ibid.*, p. 226.

11 Marta Russell, "Targeting Disability," *Monthly Review*, vol. 56, no. 11 (April 2005).

12 Peter A. Diamond and Peter R. Orszag, *Saving Social Security: A Balanced Approach.* Washington, D.C.: Brookings Institution Press, 2004, p. 48.

Point: Social Security Does More Harm Than Good

1 Michael Kinsley, "Grandfather-Clause Politics," Slate.com, November 6, 2003.

2 Howard Gleckman and Mike McNamee, "By Raising Its Voice, AARP Raises Questions," *BusinessWeek*, March 14, 2005.

3 The Democratic Party. *The 2008 Democratic National Platform: Renewing America's Promise.* Denver, Col., 2008, pp. 13–14. http://www.democrats.org/a/ party/platform.html.

4 Peter J. Ferrara, *Social Security: The Inherent Contradiction.* San Francisco: Cato Institute, 1980, p. 304.

5 Peter G. Peterson, *Running on Empty: How the Democratic and Republican Parties Are Bankrupting Our Future and What Americans Can Do About It.* New

York: Farrar, Straus and Giroux, 2004, p. 154.

6 Peter J. Ferrara, *Social Security: The Inherent Contradiction.* San Francisco: Cato Institute, 1980, p. 173.

7 Peter G. Peterson, *Running on Empty: How the Democratic and Republican Parties Are Bankrupting Our Future and What Americans Can Do About It.* New York: Farrar, Straus and Giroux, 2004, p. 49.

8 Peter J. Ferrara, *Social Security: The Inherent Contradiction.* San Francisco: Cato Institute, 1980, p. 213.

9 Olson is quoted in Peter G. Peterson, *Running on Empty: How the Democratic and Republican Parties Are Bankrupting Our Future and What Americans Can Do About It.* New York: Farrar, Straus and Giroux, 2004, p. 152.

10 Jagadeesh Gokhale, *The Impact of Social Security Reform on Low-Income Workers.* Washington, D.C.: Cato Institute, 2001, p. 7.

11 The council is quoted in *Weinberger v. Wiesenfeld*, 420 U.S. 636, 653 (1975), footnote 20.

12 President's Commission to Strengthen Social Security. *Strengthening Social Security and Creating Personal Wealth for All Americans.* Washington, D.C., 2001, p. 7.

Counterpoint: Social Security Helps Millions of Americans

1 Peter A. Diamond and Peter R. Orszag, *Saving Social Security: A Balanced Approach.* Washington, D.C.: Brookings Institution Press, 2004, p. 147.

2 Nancy Altman, *The Battle for Social Security: From FDR's Vision to Bush's Gamble.* Hoboken, N.J.: John Wiley & Sons, 2005, p. 96.

3 *Ibid.*, p. 312.

4 *Helvering v. Davis*, 301 U.S. 619, 642 (1937).

5 Social Security Administration. *The Future of Social Security*, 2008. Washington, D.C., 2008, p. 6.

6 Nancy Altman, *The Battle for Social Security: From FDR's Vision to Bush's Gamble.* Hoboken, N.J.: John Wiley & Sons, 2005, p. 315.

7 Paul Krugman, "Little Black Lies," *New York Times*, January 28, 2005.

8 Teresa Ghilarducci, *When I'm Sixty-Four: The Plot Against Pensions and the Plan to Save Them*. Princeton, N.J.: Princeton University Press, 2008, p. 227.

9 *Ibid.*, p. 55.

10 Dean Baker, Testimony Before the Senate Special Committee on Aging, February 25, 2009.

11 Dean Baker, "Stop Baby Boomer Bashing: Protect Social Security and Medicare," Truthout.com, May 26, 2009.

Point: Personal Accounts Are Superior to Social Security

1 Niall Ferguson, *The Ascent of Money: A Financial History of the World*. New York: The Penguin Press, 2008, p. 202.

2 Paul Kasriel, "Privatize Social Security Before I Spend Your Pension!" January 28, 2005. http://www.safehaven.com/article-2518.htm.

3 Peter J. Ferrara, *Social Security: The Inherent Contradiction*. San Francisco: Cato Institute, 1980, p. 16.

4 President's Commission to Strengthen Social Security. *Strengthening Social Security and Creating Personal Wealth for All Americans*. Washington, D.C., 2001, p. 143.

5 George P. Schultz and John B. Shoven, *Putting Our House in Order: A Guide to Social Security and Health Care Reform*. New York: W.W. Norton & Company, 2008, p. 63.

6 Peter G. Peterson, *Running on Empty: How the Democratic and Republican Parties Are Bankrupting Our Future and What Americans Can Do About It*. New York: Farrar, Straus and Giroux, 2004, p. 111.

7 Cato Institute. *Cato Handbook for Policymakers, Seventh Edition*. Washington, D.C., 2009, p. 185. http://www.cato.org/pubs/handbook/hb111.

8 Rahm Emanuel, "Supplementing Social Security," *Wall Street Journal*, September 13, 2007.

9 President's Commission to Strengthen Social Security. *Strengthening Social Security and Creating Personal Wealth for All Americans*. Washington, D.C., 2001, p. 28.

10 *Ibid.*, p. 40.

11 Niall Ferguson, *The Ascent of Money: A Financial History of the World*. New York: The Penguin Press, 2008, pp. 217–218.

12 Ray Holbrook and Alcestis "Cooky" Oberg, *Galveston County: A Model for Social Security Reform. Brief Analysis no. 514*, p. 2. Washington, D.C.: National Center for Policy Analysis, 2005.

Counterpoint: Personal Accounts Are Dangerous

1 Teresa Ghilarducci, *When I'm Sixty-Four: The Plot Against Pensions and the Plan to Save Them*. Princeton, N.J.: Princeton University Press, 2008, p. 178.

2 The Century Foundation, *Chile's Privatization Failures*. New York, 2005. http://www.tcf.org/Publications/RetirementSecurity/chilefactsheet.pdf.

3 Dean Baker, Testimony Before the Senate Special Committee on Aging, February 25, 2009.

4 Teresa Ghilarducci, *When I'm Sixty-Four: The Plot Against Pensions and the Plan to Save Them*. Princeton, N.J.: Princeton University Press, 2008, p. 155.

5 *Ibid.*, p. 102.

6 Dean Baker, "The Peter G. Peterson Crew Is Coming After Your Social Security and Medicare," *The Guardian* (UK), February 23, 2009.

7 Teresa Ghilarducci, *When I'm Sixty-Four: The Plot Against Pensions and the Plan to Save Them*. Princeton, N.J.: Princeton University Press, 2008, p. 163.

8 Norquist is quoted in Robert Dreyfuss, "Grover Norquist: 'Field Marshal' of the Bush Plan," *The Nation*, April 26, 2001.

9 Peter A. Diamond and Peter R. Orszag, *Saving Social Security: A Balanced Approach*. Washington, D.C.: Brookings Institution Press, 2004, p. 175.

10 Marta Russell, "Targeting Disability," *Monthly Review*, vol. 56, no. 11 (April 2005).

Conclusion: Social Security's Future

1 President's Commission to Strengthen Social Security. *Strengthening Social*

Security and Creating Personal Wealth for All Americans. Washington, D.C., 2001, p. 5.

2 Cato Institute. *Cato Handbook for Policymakers, Seventh Edition.* Washington, D.C., 2009, p. 181. http://www.cato.org/pubs/handbook/hb111.

3 Paul D. Ryan, "A GOP Road Map for America's Future," *Wall Street Journal,* January 26, 2010.

4 Jackie Calmes, "Democrats Resisting Obama on Social Security," *New York Times,* February 23, 2009.

5 Peter G. Peterson, *Running on Empty: How the Democratic and Republican Parties Are Bankrupting Our Future and What Americans Can Do About It.* New York: Farrar, Straus and Giroux, 2004, pp. 23–24.

6 Laurence J. Kotlikoff, "Is the United States Bankrupt," *Federal Reserve Bank of St. Louis Review,* July/August 2006, p. 242.

7 *Ibid.,* p. 237.

8 Teresa Ghilarducci, *When I'm Sixty-Four: The Plot Against Pensions and*

the Plan to Save Them. Princeton, N.J.: Princeton University Press, 2008, p. 145.

9 Peter J. Ferrara, *Social Security: The Inherent Contradiction.* San Francisco: Cato Institute, 1980, p. 207.

10 Teresa Ghilarducci, *When I'm Sixty-Four: The Plot Against Pensions and the Plan to Save Them.* Princeton, N.J.: Princeton University Press, 2008, p. 56.

11 President's Commission to Strengthen Social Security. *Strengthening Social Security and Creating Personal Wealth for All Americans.* Washington, D.C., 2001, p. 64.

12 Cato Institute. *Cato Handbook for Policymakers, Seventh Edition.* Washington, D.C., 2009, p. 186. http://www.cato.org/pubs/handbook/hb111.

13 Robert J. Samuelson, "Let Them Go Bankrupt, Soon: Solving Social Security and Medicare," *Newsweek,* June 1, 2009.

14 Executive Order No. 13531, National Commission on Fiscal Responsibility and Reform, *Federal Register* vol. 75, p. 7927 (February 23, 2010).

Books

Altman, Nancy. *The Battle for Social Security: From FDR's Vision to Bush's Gamble.* Hoboken, N.J.: John Wiley & Sons, 2005.

Diamond, Peter A., and Peter R. Orszag. *Saving Social Security: A Balanced Approach.* Washington, D.C.: Brookings Institution Press, 2004.

Ghilarducci, Teresa. *When I'm Sixty-Four: The Plot Against Pensions and the Plan to Save Them.* Princeton, N.J.: Princeton University Press, 2008.

Peterson, Peter G. *Running on Empty: How the Democratic and Republican Parties Are Bankrupting Our Future and What Americans Can Do About It.* New York: Farrar, Straus and Giroux, 2004.

Schultz, George P., and John B. Shoven. *Putting Our House in Order: A Guide to Social Security and Health Care Reform.* New York: W.W. Norton & Company, 2008.

Web Sites

AARP
http://www.aarp.org
This is an advocacy organization for older Americans. It has more than 40 million members, all over the age of 50. AARP was a prominent opponent of President Bush's proposal to make personal accounts a part of Social Security.

American Enterprise Institute for Public Policy Research
http://www.aei.org
Established in 1943, this is a research and educational institute dedicated to "expanding liberty, increasing individual opportunity, and strengthening free enterprise."

Cato Institute
http://www.cato.org
Social Security reform has been a priority of the Cato Institute, a public policy research foundation that favors limited government, free markets, and individual liberty.

Concord Coalition
http://www.concordcoalition.org
Established in 1992 by members of both major parties, it advocates for a "generationally responsible fiscal policy." It believes that Social Security in its current form is unsustainable. Peter G. Peterson, a prominent advocate of reform, was one of this organization's founders.

National Committee to Preserve Social Security and Medicare

http://www.ncpssm.org

Founded in 1982 by James Roosevelt, son of President Franklin D. Roosevelt, it calls itself the nation's leading advocacy group for Social Security and Medicare.

The Pension Rights Center

http://www.pensionrights.org

Established in 1976 to protect and promote the retirement security of American workers and retirees, the center's board of directors is chaired by Nancy Altman, the author of *The Battle for Social Security*, who supports Social Security in its present form.

Social Security Administration

http://www.socialsecurity.gov

The Social Security Administration is an independent federal agency that oversees the Social Security system. The SSA is headed by a commissioner appointed by the president. A board of trustees oversees the Social Security system's Old Age and Survivors Insurance and Disability Insurance trust funds. Payroll taxes and other revenue taken by the Social Security system go into the trust funds, and benefits are paid out of those funds. In 1994, Congress created a seven-member, bipartisan Social Security Advisory Board, which makes suggestions for improving the system.

PICTURE CREDITS

PAGE

14: The Granger Collection, NYC
19: Francis Miller/Time Life Pictures/Getty Images
33: Bock/MCT/Newscom

42: The Granger Collection, NYC
80: Staff/MCT/Newscom
106: Treible/MCT/Newscom

CONTRIBUTORS ||||▷

PAUL RUSCHMANN, J.D., is a legal analyst and writer based in Canton, Michigan. He received his undergraduate degree from the University of Notre Dame and his law degree from the University of Michigan. He is a member of the State Bar of Michigan. His areas of specialization include legislation, public safety, traffic and transportation, and trade regulation. He is also the author of 15 other books in the POINT/COUNTERPOINT series, which deal with such issues as the military draft, indecency in the media, private property rights, the War on Terror, and global warming. He can be found online at www.PaulRuschmann.com.

MARYANNE NASIATKA is a writer and researcher based in southeastern Michigan. She received an undergraduate degree in economics from the University of Notre Dame. She is a co-owner of a consulting firm that provides legislative analysis to Fortune 500 companies and industry trade associations. She was co-author of another book in the POINT/ COUNTERPOINT series, *Private Property Rights.*

ALAN MARZILLI, M.A., J.D., lives in Birmingham, Ala., and is a program associate with Advocates for Human Potential, Inc., a research and consulting firm based in Sudbury, Mass., and Albany, N.Y. He primarily works on developing training and educational materials for agencies of the federal government on topics such as housing, mental health policy, employment, and transportation. He has spoken on mental health issues in 30 states, the District of Columbia, and Puerto Rico; his work has included training mental health administrators, nonprofit management and staff, and people with mental illnesses and their families on a wide variety of topics, including effective advocacy, community-based mental health services, and housing. He has written several handbooks and training curricula that are used nationally and as far away as the territory of Guam. He managed statewide and national mental health advocacy programs and worked for several public interest lobbying organizations while studying law at Georgetown University. He has written more than a dozen books, including numerous titles in the POINT/COUNTERPOINT series.